my new fighting technique is unstoppable

my new fighting technique is unstoppable

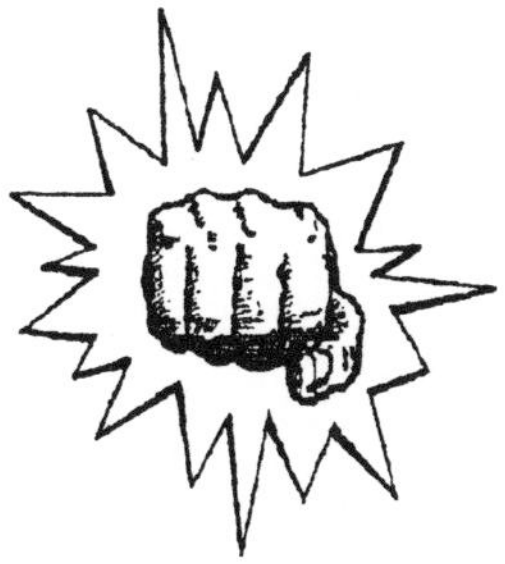

david rees

Riverhead Books
New York

Riverhead Books
Published by The Berkley Publishing Group
A division of Penguin Group (USA) Inc.
375 Hudson Street
New York, New York 10014

First Riverhead trade paperback edition: October 2003

Library of Congress Cataloging-in-Publication Data

Rees, David, 1972–
   My new fighting technique is unstoppable / David Rees.—1st Riverhead trade pbk. ed.
      p. cm.
   ISBN 1-57322-373-5
    I. Title.

   PN6727.R384M9 2003
   741.5973—dc21

                                        2003047004

Printed in the United States of America
10   9   8   7   6   5   4   3   2   1

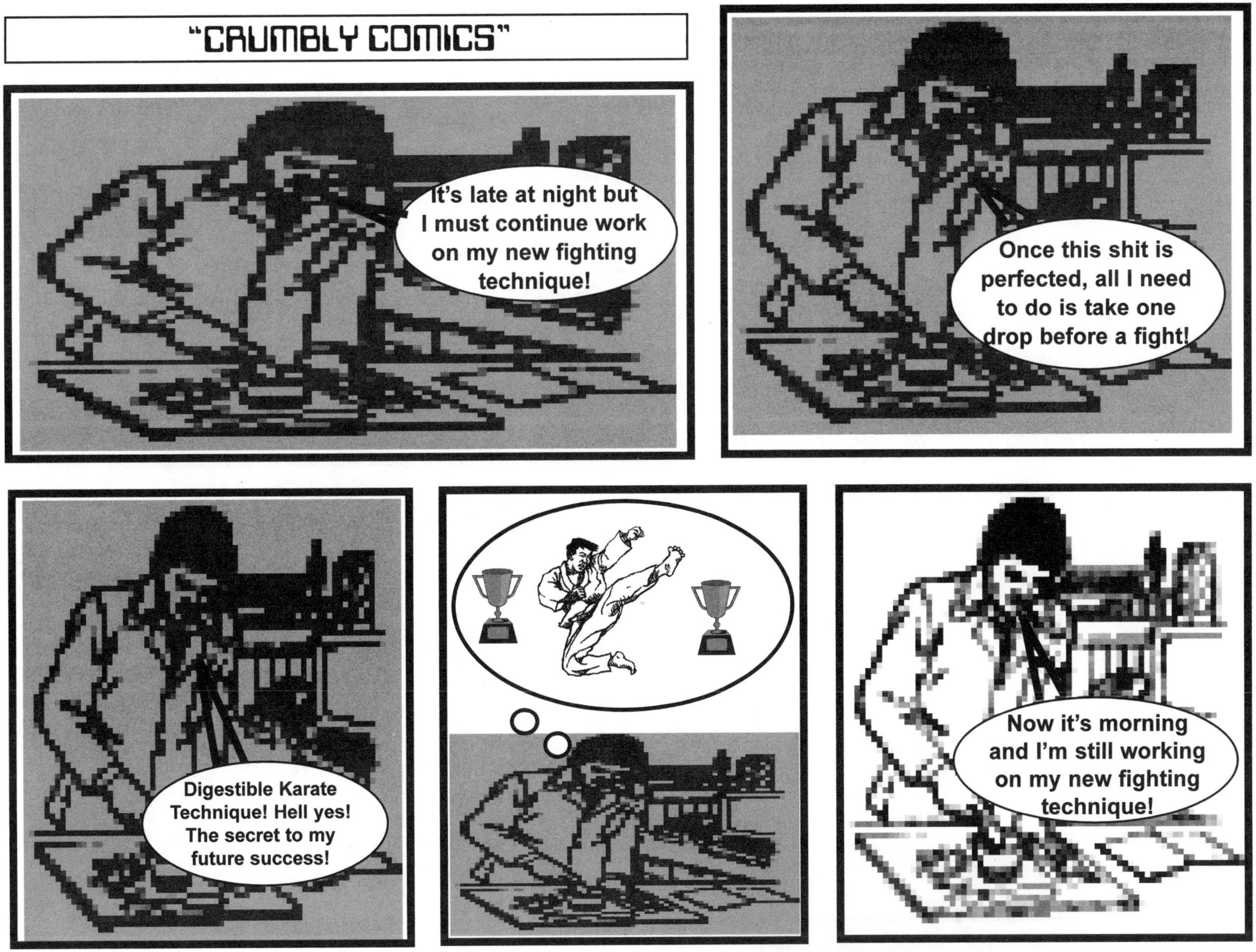
"CRUMBLY COMICS"
It's late at night but I must continue work on my new fighting technique!
Once this shit is perfected, all I need to do is take one drop before a fight!
Digestible Karate Technique! Hell yes! The secret to my future success!
Now it's morning and I'm still working on my new fighting technique!

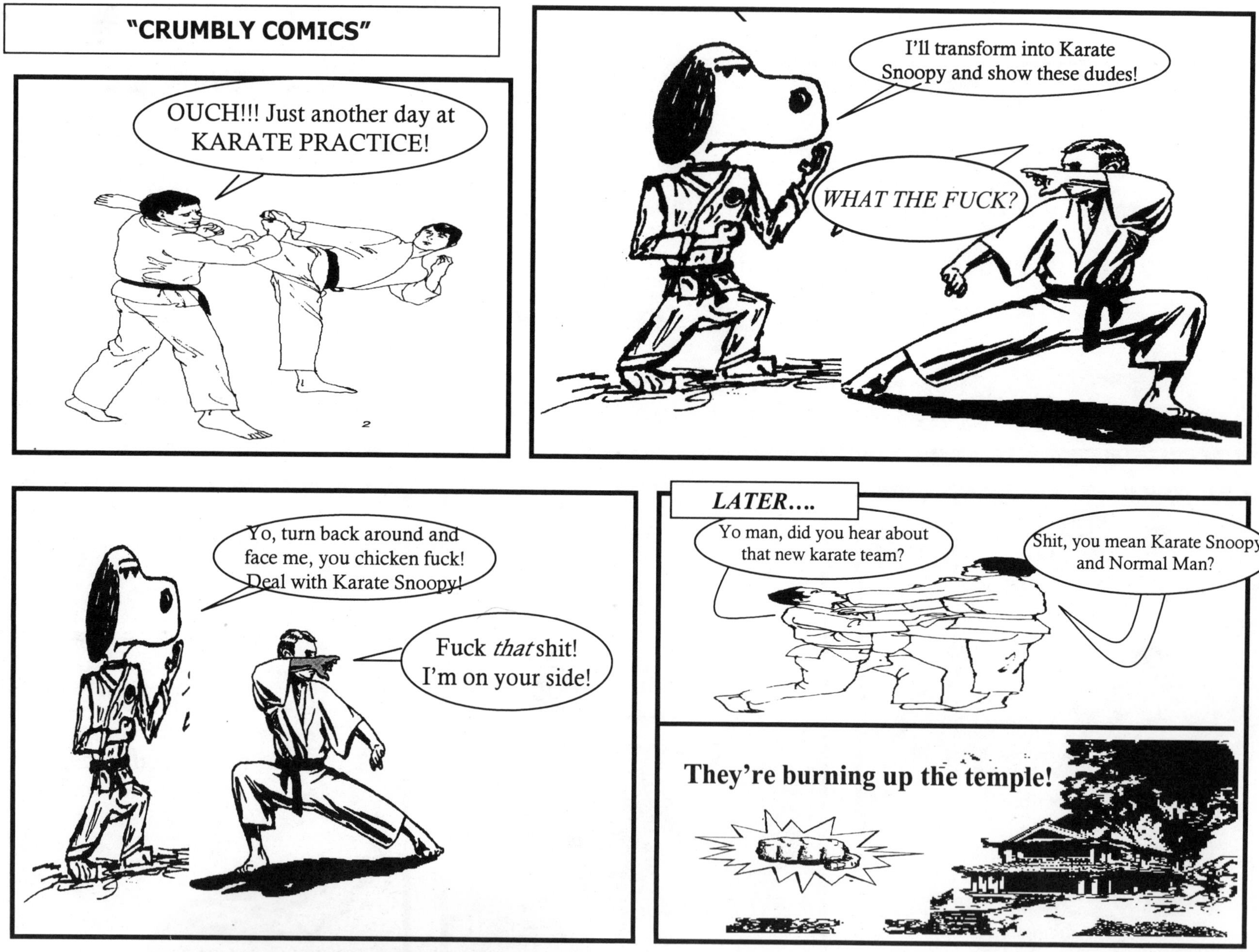
"CRUMBLY COMICS"
OUCH!!! Just another day at KARATE PRACTICE!
I'll transform into Karate Snoopy and show these dudes!
WHAT THE FUCK?
Yo, turn back around and face me, you chicken fuck! Deal with Karate Snoopy!
Fuck *that* shit! I'm on your side!
LATER....
Yo man, did you hear about that new karate team?
Shit, you mean Karate Snoopy and Normal Man?
They're burning up the temple!

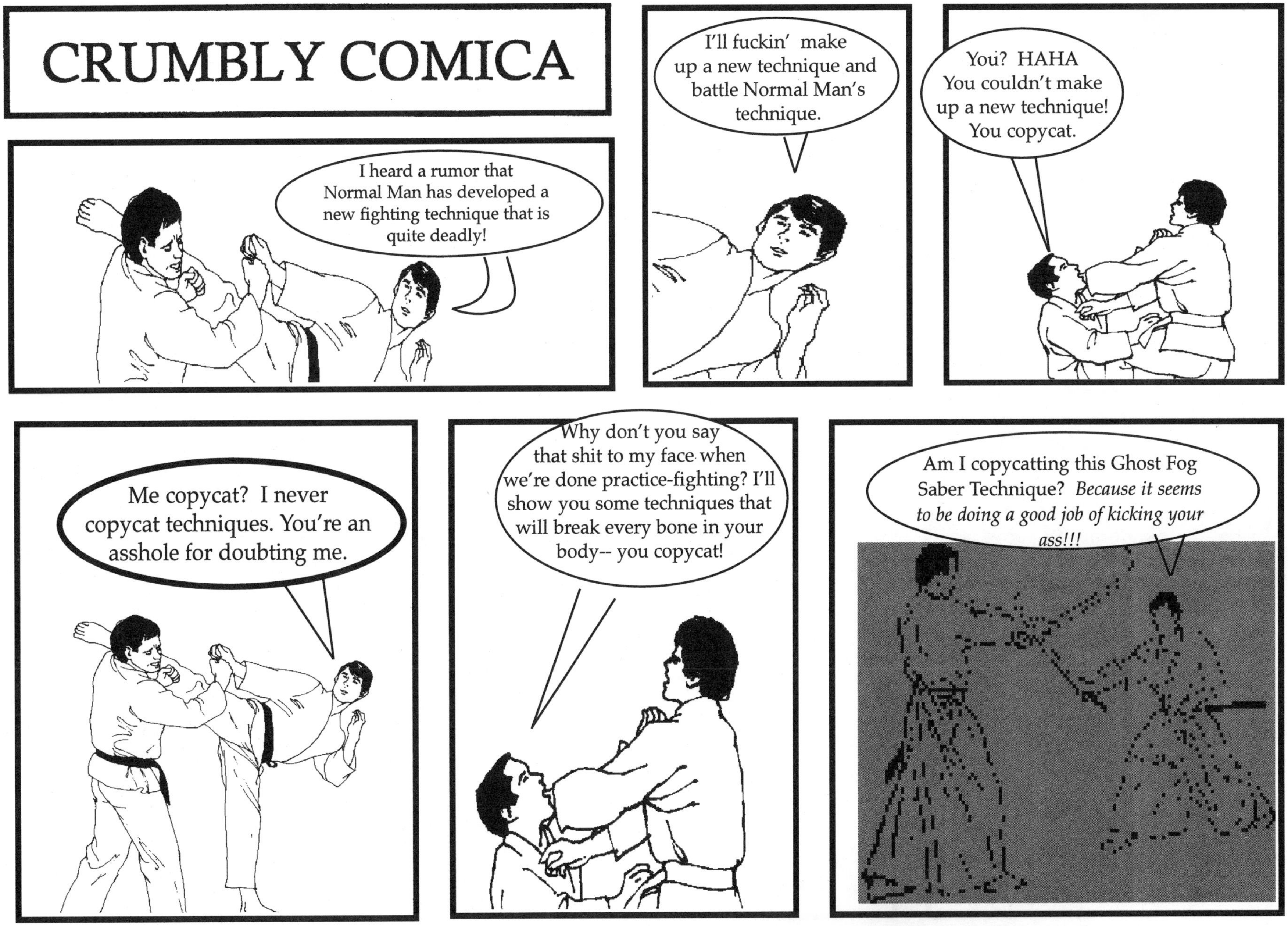
CRUMBLY COMICA
I heard a rumor that Normal Man has developed a new fighting technique that is quite deadly!
I'll fuckin' make up a new technique and battle Normal Man's technique.
You? HAHA You couldn't make up a new technique! You copycat.
Me copycat? I never copycat techniques. You're an asshole for doubting me.
Why don't you say that shit to my face when we're done practice-fighting? I'll show you some techniques that will break every bone in your body-- you copycat!
Am I copycatting this Ghost Fog Saber Technique? *Because it seems to be doing a good job of kicking your ass!!!*

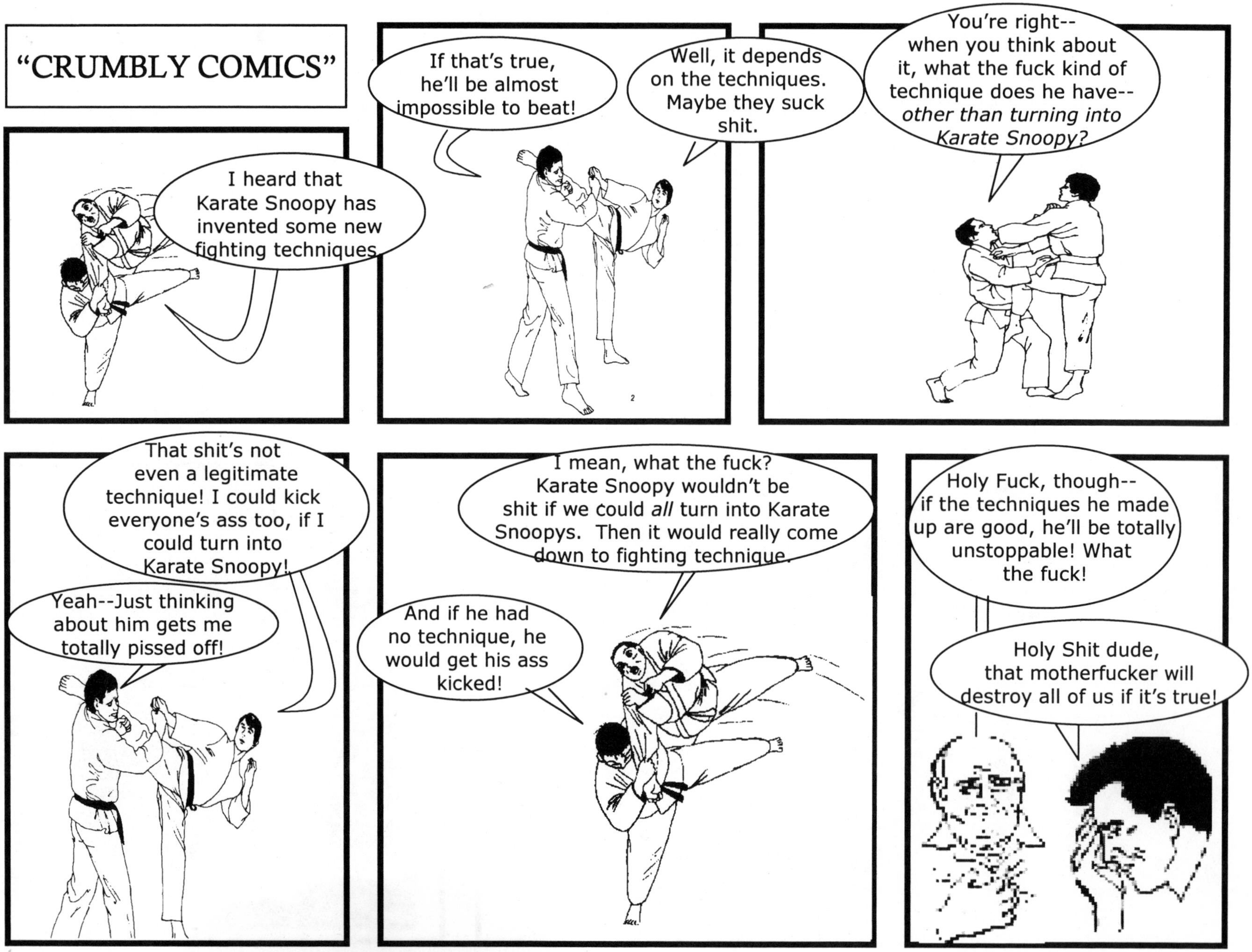
"CRUMBLY COMICS"
I heard that Karate Snoopy has invented some new fighting techniques
If that's true, he'll be almost impossible to beat!
Well, it depends on the techniques. Maybe they suck shit.
You're right-- when you think about it, what the fuck kind of technique does he have-- *other than turning into Karate Snoopy?*
That shit's not even a legitimate technique! I could kick everyone's ass too, if I could turn into Karate Snoopy!
Yeah--Just thinking about him gets me totally pissed off!
I mean, what the fuck? Karate Snoopy wouldn't be shit if we could *all* turn into Karate Snoopys. Then it would really come down to fighting technique.
And if he had no technique, he would get his ass kicked!
Holy Fuck, though-- if the techniques he made up are good, he'll be totally unstoppable! What the fuck!
Holy Shit dude, that motherfucker will destroy all of us if it's true!

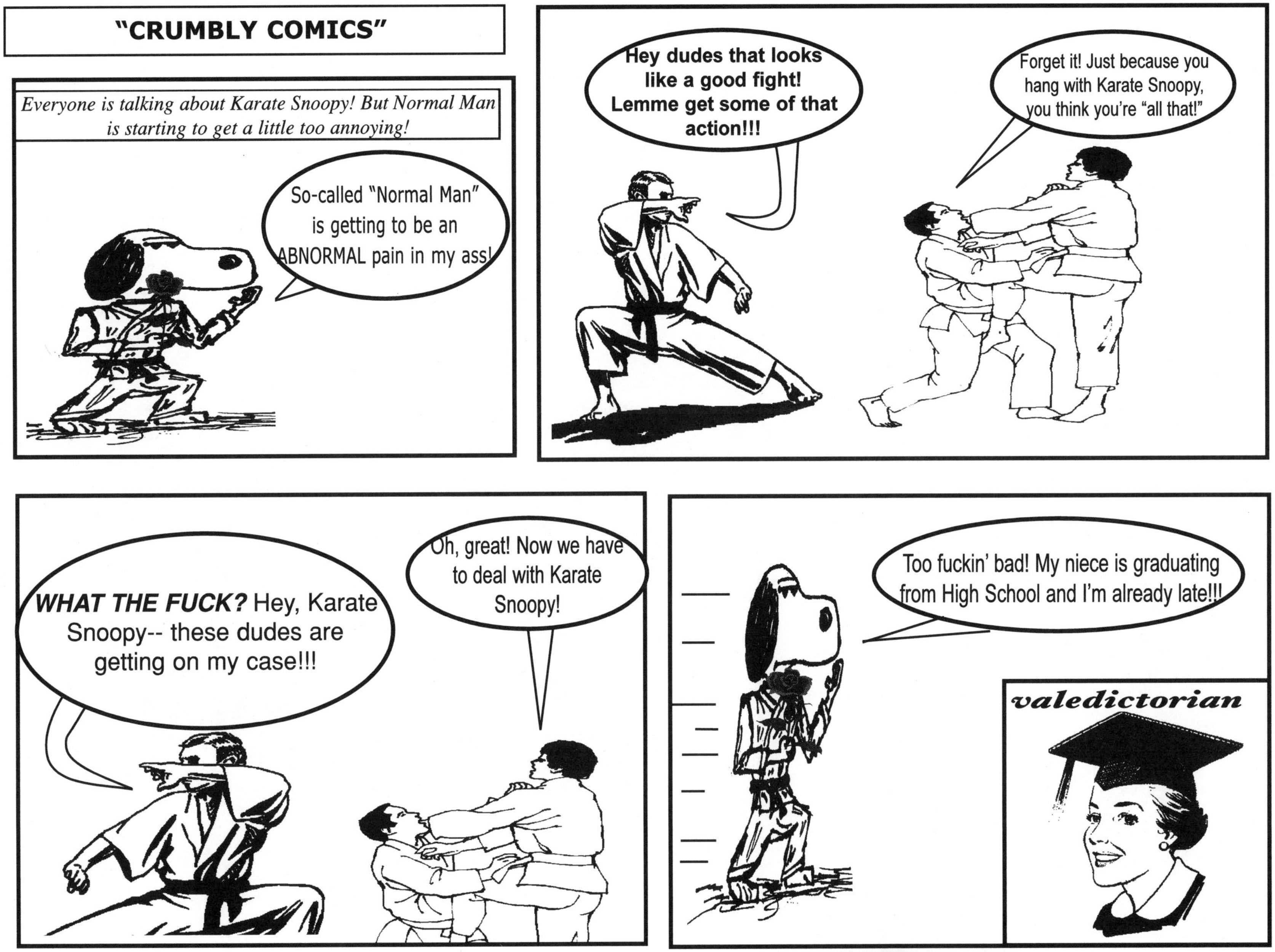
"CRUMBLY COMICS"
Everyone is talking about Karate Snoopy! But Normal Man is starting to get a little too annoying!
So-called "Normal Man" is getting to be an ABNORMAL pain in my ass!
Hey dudes that looks like a good fight! Lemme get some of that action!!!
Forget it! Just because you hang with Karate Snoopy, you think you're "all that!"
WHAT THE FUCK? Hey, Karate Snoopy-- these dudes are getting on my case!!!
Oh, great! Now we have to deal with Karate Snoopy!
Too fuckin' bad! My niece is graduating from High School and I'm already late!!!
valedictorian

"CRUMBLY COMICS"

Where the hell is Karate Snoopy? Is he avoiding me?

I'll fuckin' turn against him and defeat him in practice-fighting OR regular fighting! Then my intimidation factor will increase!!!

Karate Snoopy! Show your face, so I can stick my fucking foot in it!

swooosh

Ah HA! There you are! Motherfucker, come over here and receive my knuckles in your facial region!

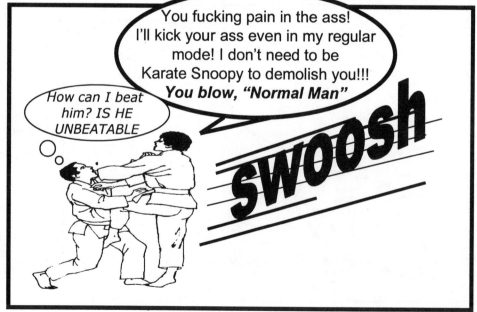

You fucking pain in the ass! I'll kick your ass even in my regular mode! I don't need to be Karate Snoopy to demolish you!!! *You blow, "Normal Man"*

How can I beat him? IS HE UNBEATABLE

SWOOSH

CRUMBLY COMICS

I heard a rumor that Normal Man has developed a new cancer disease that is quite deadly!

I'll fuckin' make up a cancer cure and battle Normal Man's disease.

You? HAHA! You couldn't make up a cancer cure! *Don't ask me why I say this.*

Doubting Thomas, eh? Do you doubt that I'm kicking you in the goddamn face right now?

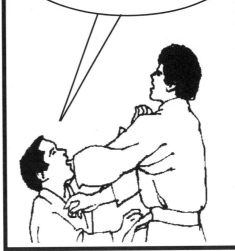

Listen-- remember how I didn't want you to ask me why I don't think you can make up a cancer cure? I've changed my mind-- I'll tell you why.

You can't make up a cancer cure due to my Ghost Fog Saber Technique-- (which is a cure for your disease of Not Getting Enough Ass Kicking)

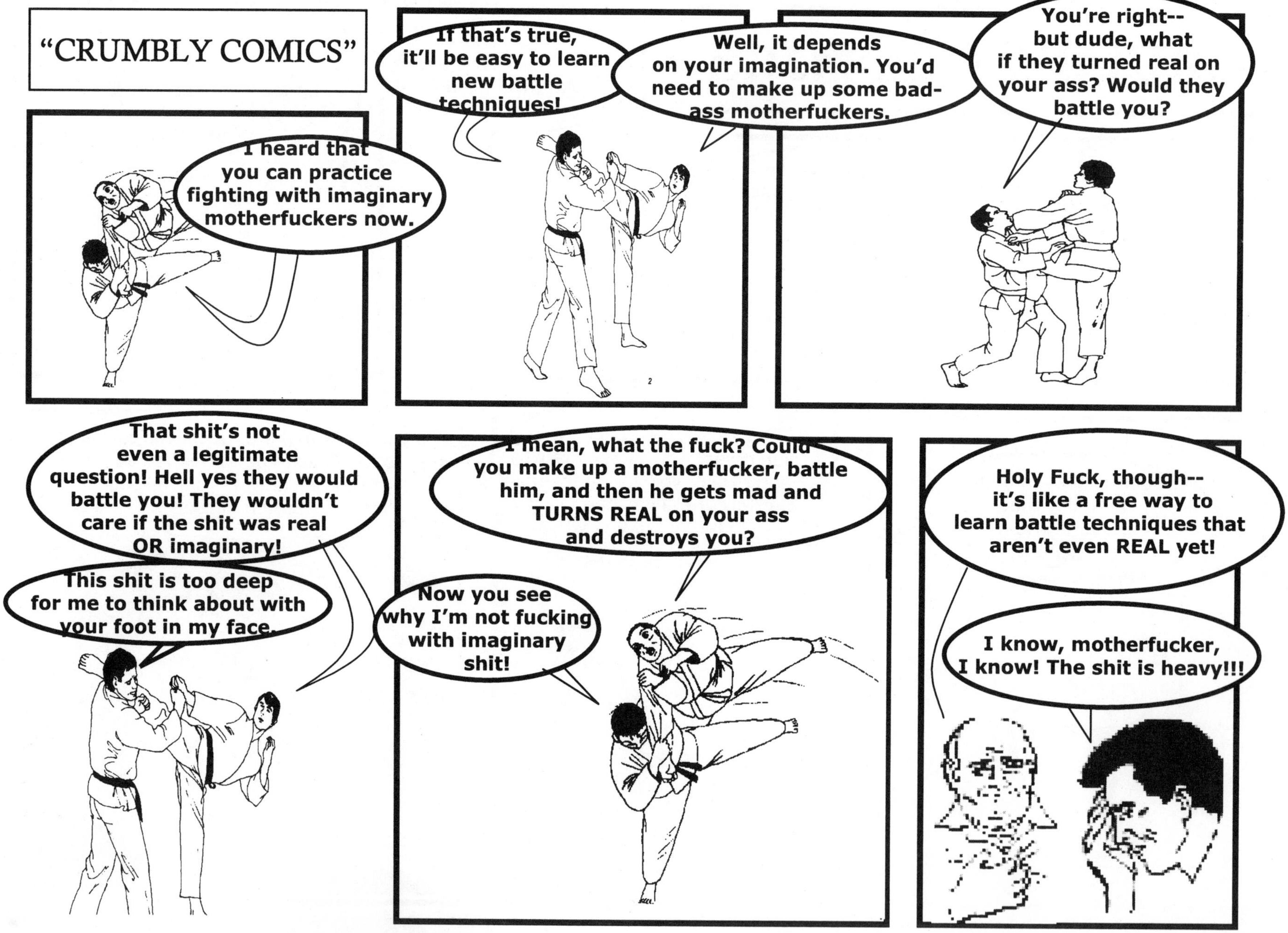
"CRUMBLY COMICS"
I heard that you can practice fighting with imaginary motherfuckers now.
If that's true, it'll be easy to learn new battle techniques!
Well, it depends on your imagination. You'd need to make up some bad-ass motherfuckers.
You're right--but dude, what if they turned real on your ass? Would they battle you?
That shit's not even a legitimate question! Hell yes they would battle you! They wouldn't care if the shit was real OR imaginary!
This shit is too deep for me to think about with your foot in my face.
I mean, what the fuck? Could you make up a motherfucker, battle him, and then he gets mad and TURNS REAL on your ass and destroys you?
Now you see why I'm not fucking with imaginary shit!
Holy Fuck, though--it's like a free way to learn battle techniques that aren't even REAL yet!
I know, motherfucker, I know! The shit is heavy!!!

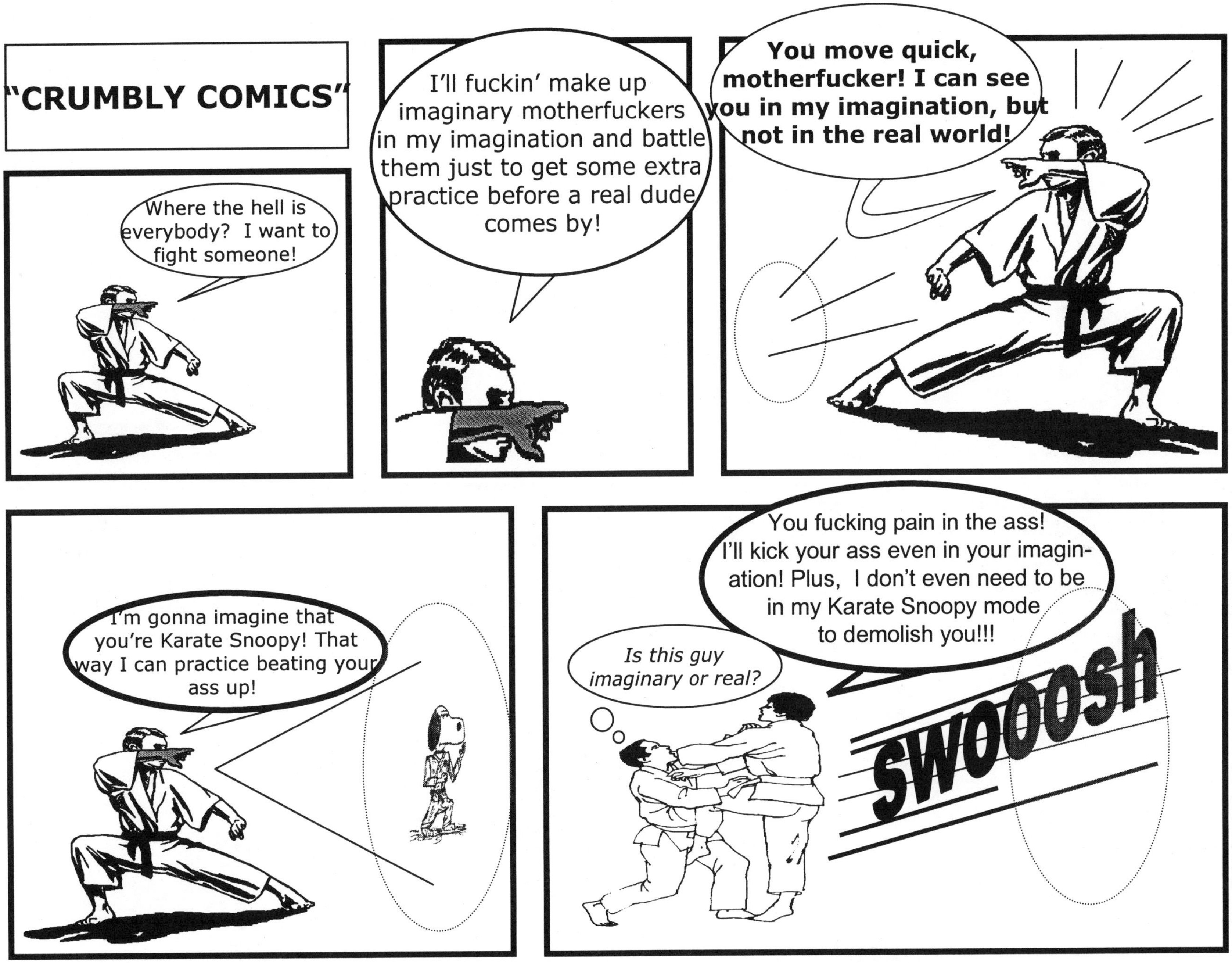
"CRUMBLY COMICS"
Where the hell is everybody? I want to fight someone!
I'll fuckin' make up imaginary motherfuckers in my imagination and battle them just to get some extra practice before a real dude comes by!
You move quick, motherfucker! I can see you in my imagination, but not in the real world!
I'm gonna imagine that you're Karate Snoopy! That way I can practice beating your ass up!
You fucking pain in the ass! I'll kick your ass even in your imagin-ation! Plus, I don't even need to be in my Karate Snoopy mode to demolish you!!!
Is this guy imaginary or real?
SWOOOSH

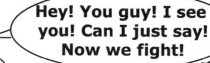

"CRUMBLY COMICS"

Hi! I'm new to this temple! Can I just say one thing! I will fight anyone here!

Hey! You guy! I see you! Can I just say! Now we fight!

This dude doesn't sound well! Should I fight him?

What is that! Your technique! It is very shaky! Are you ready for me!

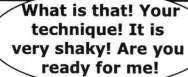

I have to say! What style do you have! I don't know what I am seeing! I am leaving this temple!

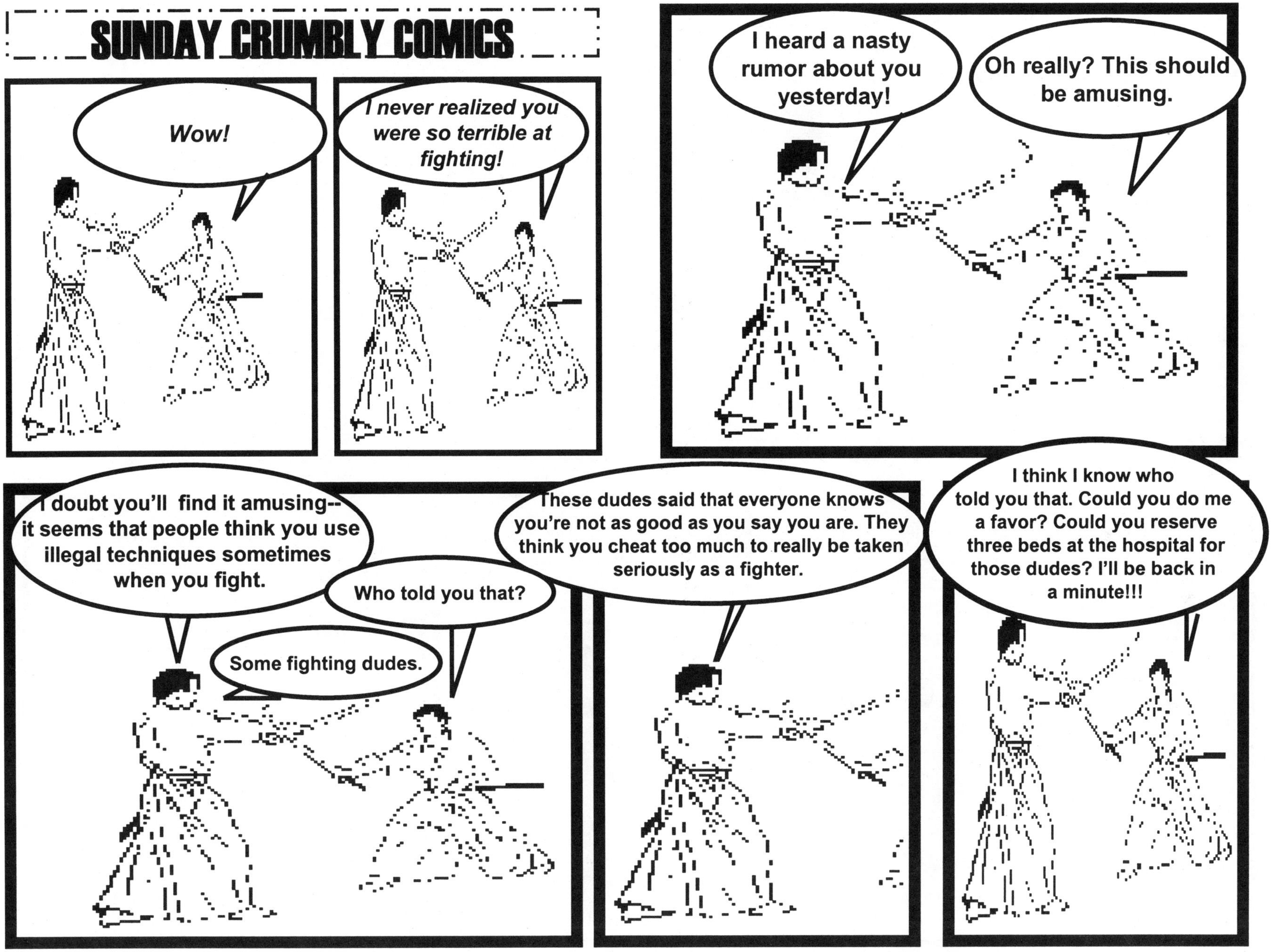
SUNDAY CRUMBLY COMICS
Wow!
I never realized you were so terrible at fighting!
I heard a nasty rumor about you yesterday!
Oh really? This should be amusing.
I doubt you'll find it amusing-- it seems that people think you use illegal techniques sometimes when you fight.
Who told you that?
Some fighting dudes.
These dudes said that everyone knows you're not as good as you say you are. They think you cheat too much to really be taken seriously as a fighter.
I think I know who told you that. Could you do me a favor? Could you reserve three beds at the hospital for those dudes? I'll be back in a minute!!!

"CRUMBLY COMICS"
Goddamn this is some thick fog!
How am I supposed to battle motherfuckers I can't even see?
You're trapped in my Mental Fog Box! I'm gonna tear you up with this shit!!!
OH SHIT!
I can break out of this shit if I just concentrate hard enough!!! Urgghh, come on, do it motherfucker!
What the fuck! You're turning see-through!!!
Oh yeah! Does anybody feel like messing with a see-through motherfucker?
Fuck that shit!

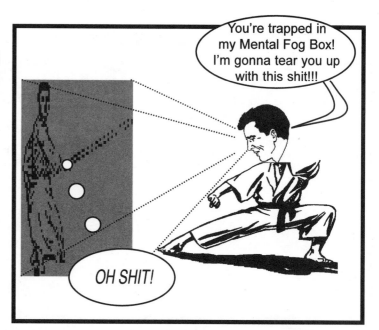

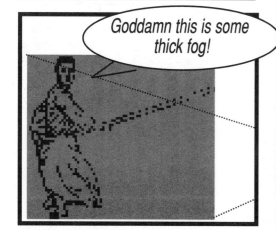

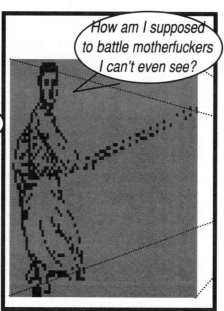

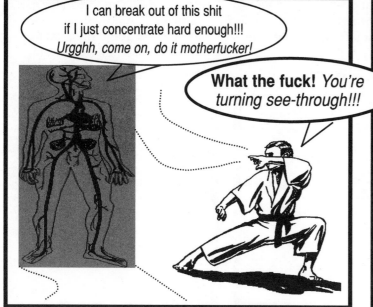

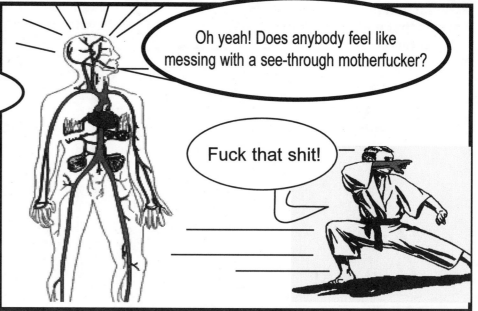

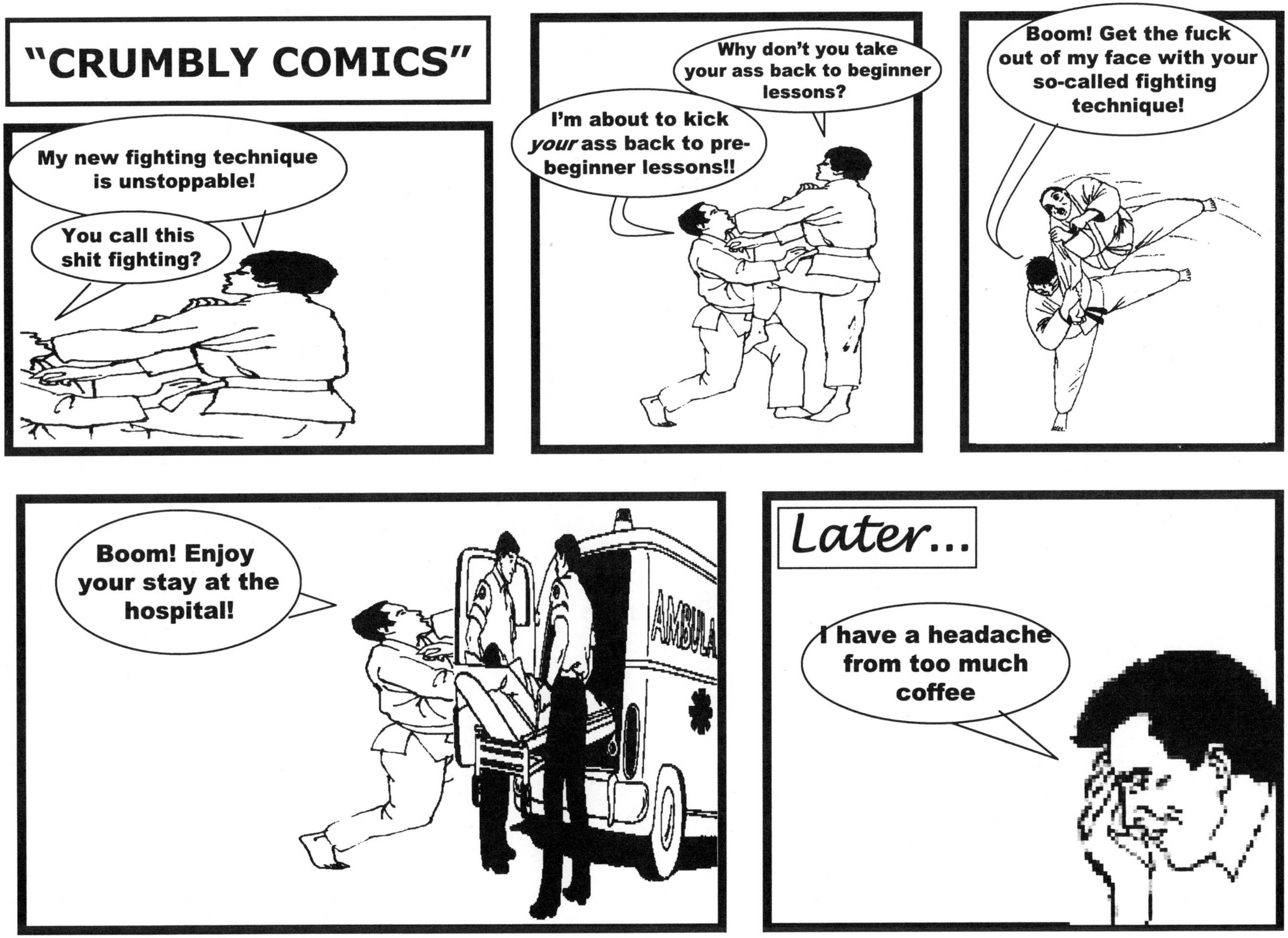
"CRUMBLY COMICS"
My new fighting technique is unstoppable!
You call this shit fighting?
Why don't you take your ass back to beginner lessons?
I'm about to kick *your* ass back to pre-beginner lessons!!
Boom! Get the fuck out of my face with your so-called fighting technique!
Boom! Enjoy your stay at the hospital!
AMBULA
Later...
I have a headache from too much coffee

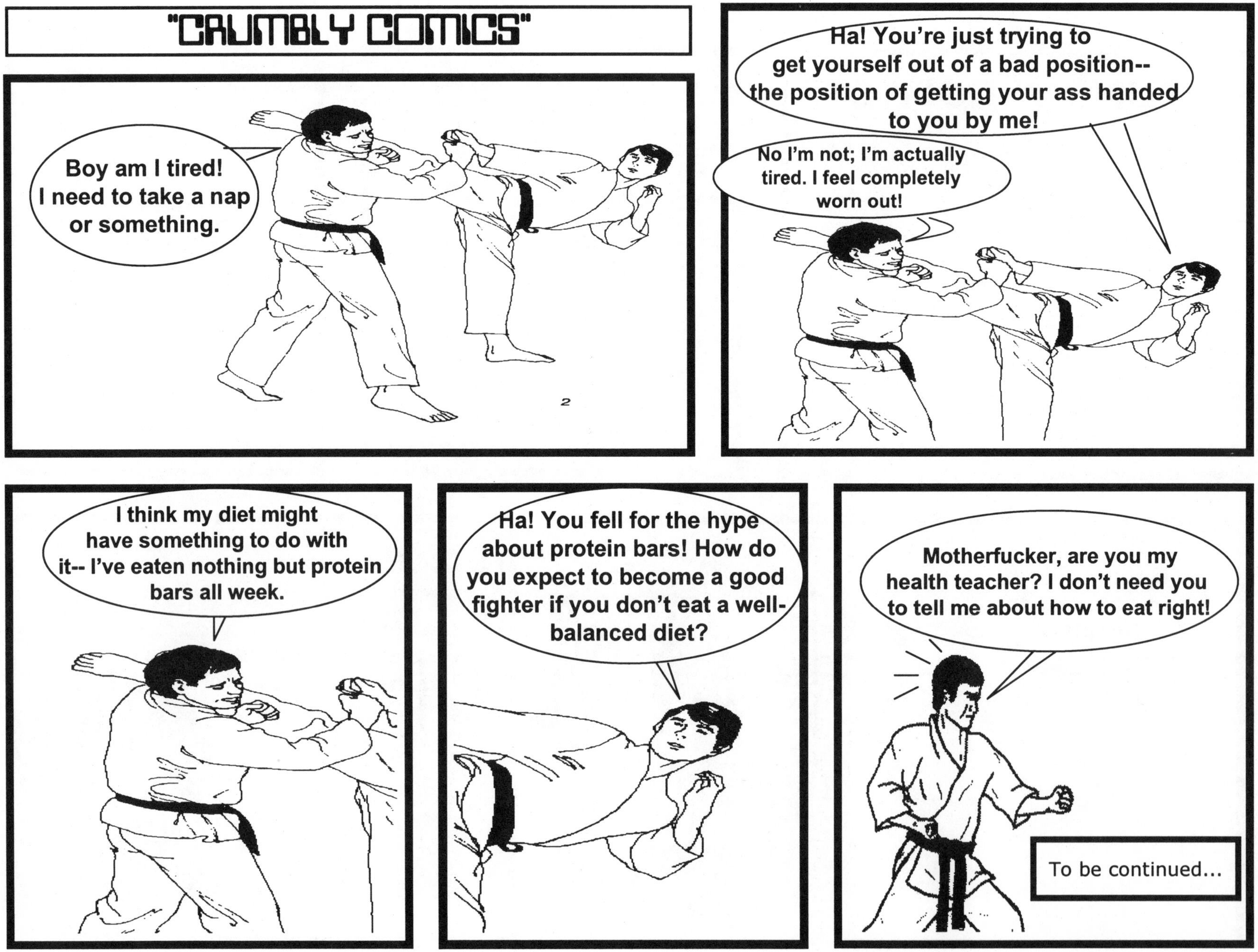
"CRUMBLY COMICS"
Boy am I tired! I need to take a nap or something.
2
Ha! You're just trying to get yourself out of a bad position-- the position of getting your ass handed to you by me!
No I'm not; I'm actually tired. I feel completely worn out!
I think my diet might have something to do with it-- I've eaten nothing but protein bars all week.
Ha! You fell for the hype about protein bars! How do you expect to become a good fighter if you don't eat a well-balanced diet?
Motherfucker, are you my health teacher? I don't need you to tell me about how to eat right!
To be continued...

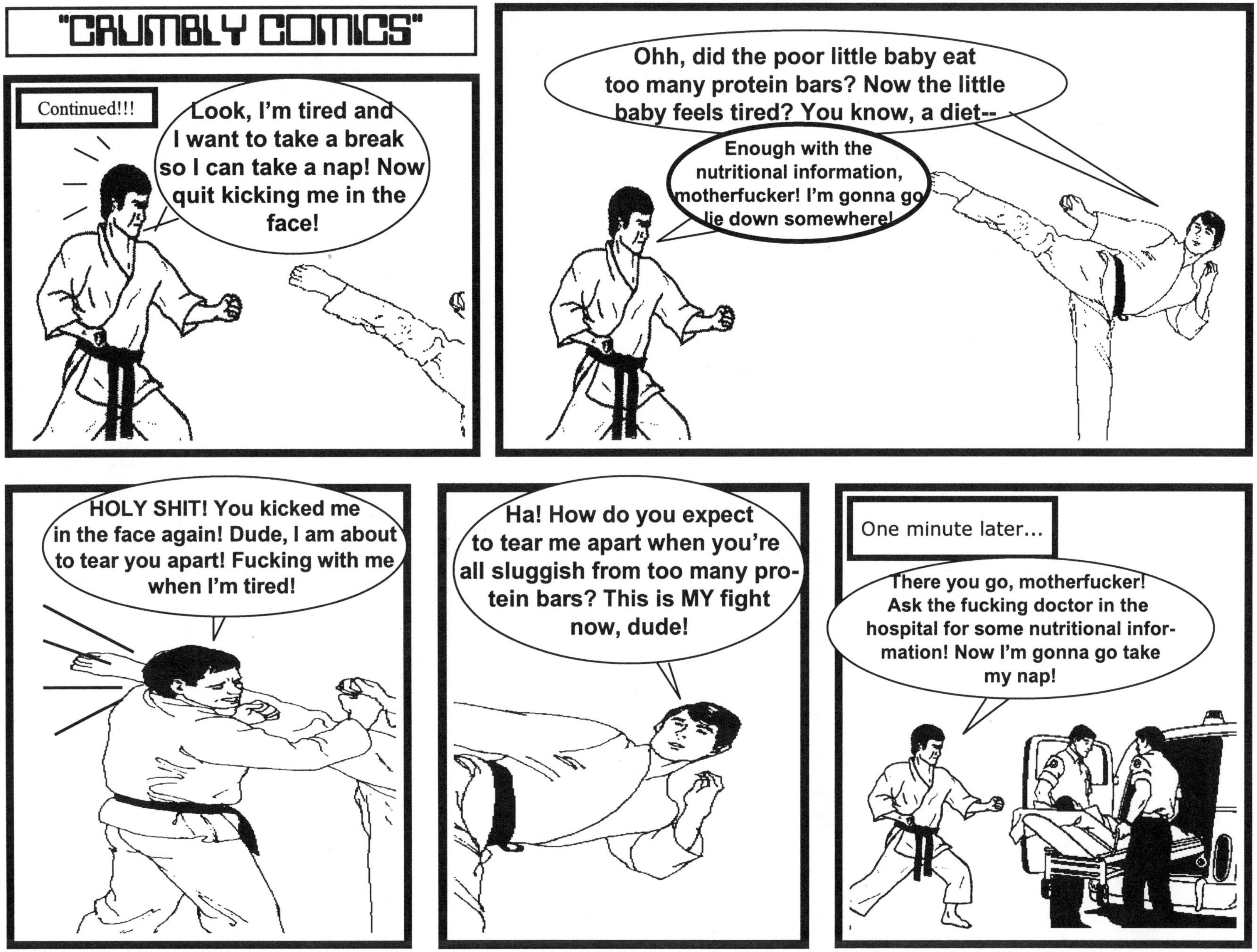
"CRUMBLY COMICS"
Continued!!!
Look, I'm tired and I want to take a break so I can take a nap! Now quit kicking me in the face!
Ohh, did the poor little baby eat too many protein bars? Now the little baby feels tired? You know, a diet--
Enough with the nutritional information, motherfucker! I'm gonna go lie down somewhere!
HOLY SHIT! You kicked me in the face again! Dude, I am about to tear you apart! Fucking with me when I'm tired!
Ha! How do you expect to tear me apart when you're all sluggish from too many protein bars? This is MY fight now, dude!
One minute later...
There you go, motherfucker! Ask the fucking doctor in the hospital for some nutritional information! Now I'm gonna go take my nap!

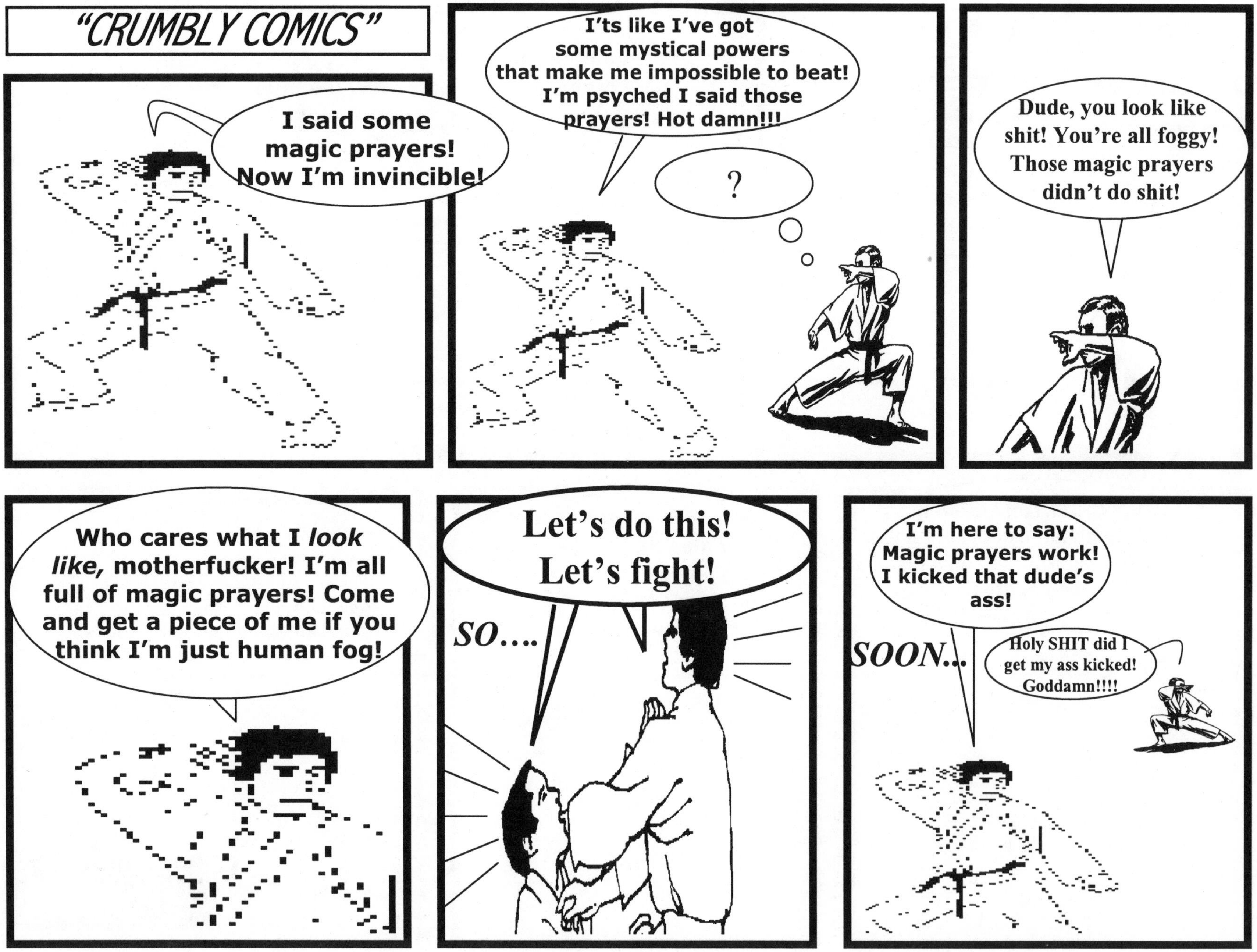
"CRUMBLY COMICS"
I said some magic prayers! Now I'm invincible!
I'ts like I've got some mystical powers that make me impossible to beat! I'm psyched I said those prayers! Hot damn!!!
?
Dude, you look like shit! You're all foggy! Those magic prayers didn't do shit!
Who cares what I *look like,* motherfucker! I'm all full of magic prayers! Come and get a piece of me if you think I'm just human fog!
SO….
Let's do this! Let's fight!
SOON…
I'm here to say: Magic prayers work! I kicked that dude's ass!
Holy SHIT did I get my ass kicked! Goddamn!!!!

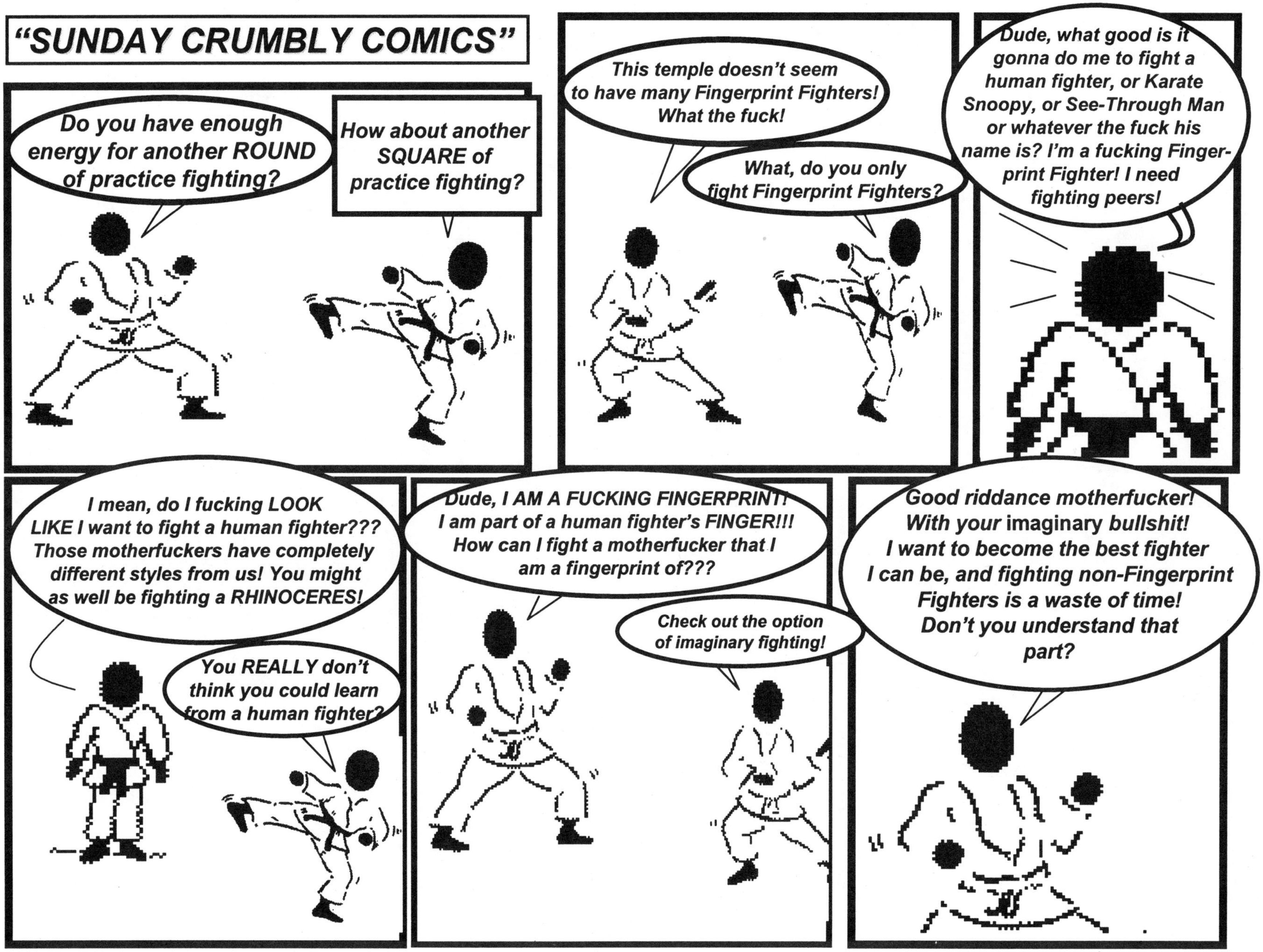
"SUNDAY CRUMBLY COMICS"
Do you have enough energy for another ROUND of practice fighting?
How about another SQUARE of practice fighting?
This temple doesn't seem to have many Fingerprint Fighters! What the fuck!
What, do you only fight Fingerprint Fighters?
Dude, what good is it gonna do me to fight a human fighter, or Karate Snoopy, or See-Through Man or whatever the fuck his name is? I'm a fucking Finger-print Fighter! I need fighting peers!
I mean, do I fucking LOOK LIKE I want to fight a human fighter??? Those motherfuckers have completely different styles from us! You might as well be fighting a RHINOCERES!
You REALLY don't think you could learn from a human fighter?
Dude, I AM A FUCKING FINGERPRINT! I am part of a human fighter's FINGER!!! How can I fight a motherfucker that I am a fingerprint of???
Check out the option of imaginary fighting!
Good riddance motherfucker! With your imaginary bullshit! I want to become the best fighter I can be, and fighting non-Fingerprint Fighters is a waste of time! Don't you understand that part?

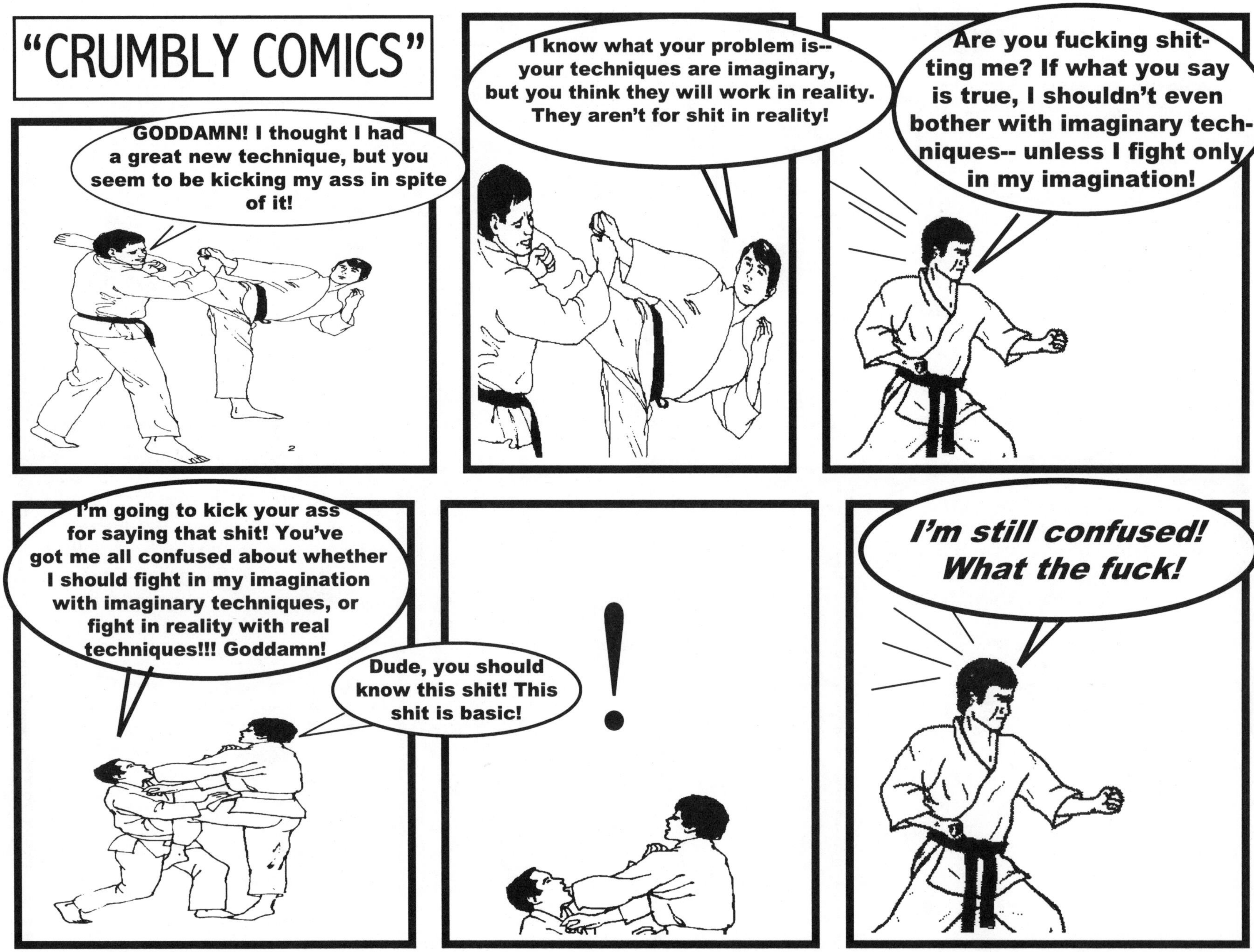
"CRUMBLY COMICS"
GODDAMN! I thought I had a great new technique, but you seem to be kicking my ass in spite of it!
I know what your problem is-- your techniques are imaginary, but you think they will work in reality. They aren't for shit in reality!
Are you fucking shitting me? If what you say is true, I shouldn't even bother with imaginary techniques-- unless I fight only in my imagination!
I'm going to kick your ass for saying that shit! You've got me all confused about whether I should fight in my imagination with imaginary techniques, or fight in reality with real techniques!!! Goddamn!
Dude, you should know this shit! This shit is basic!
!
I'm still confused! What the fuck!

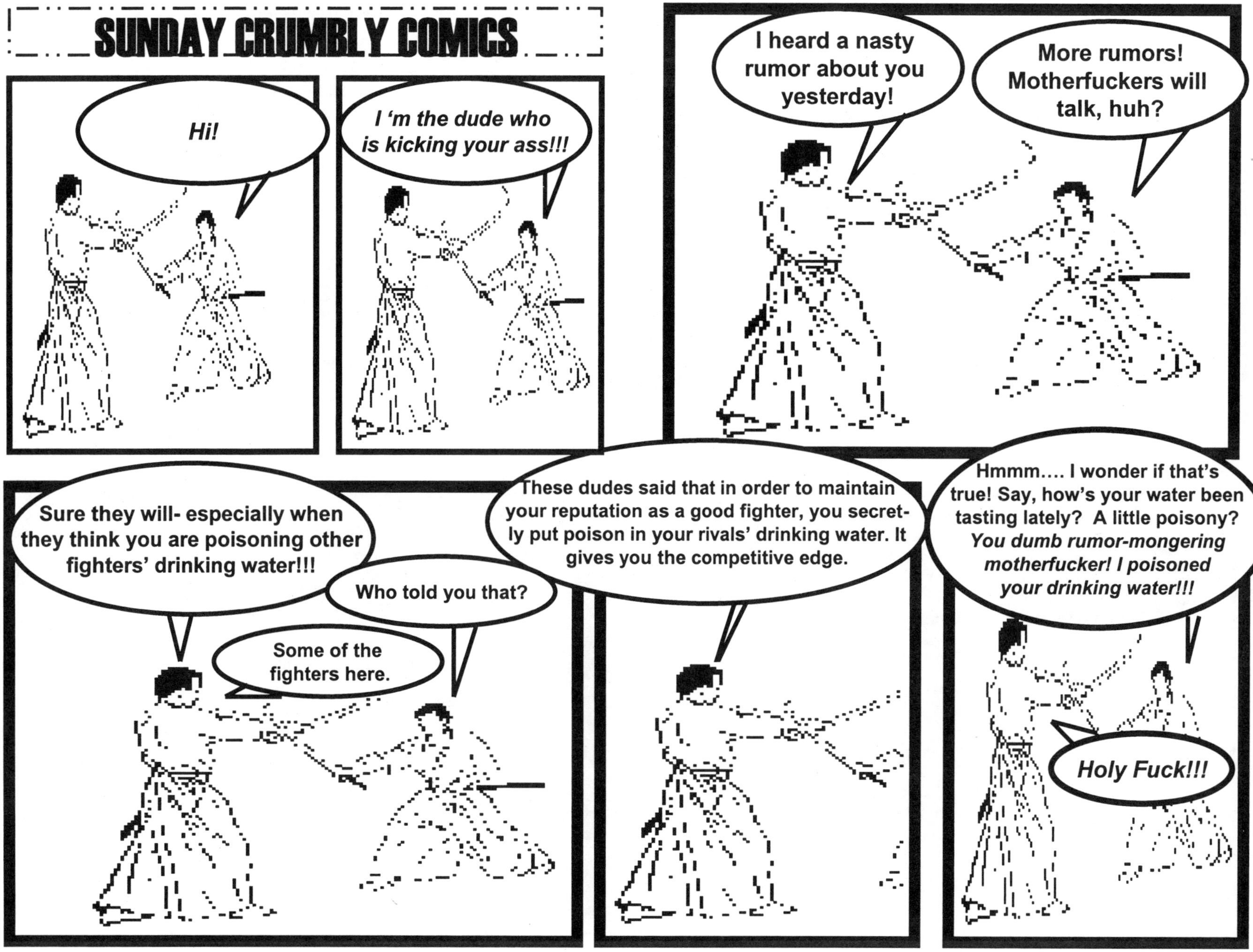
SUNDAY CRUMBLY COMICS
Hi!
I 'm the dude who is kicking your ass!!!
I heard a nasty rumor about you yesterday!
More rumors! Motherfuckers will talk, huh?
Sure they will- especially when they think you are poisoning other fighters' drinking water!!!
Who told you that?
Some of the fighters here.
These dudes said that in order to maintain your reputation as a good fighter, you secret-ly put poison in your rivals' drinking water. It gives you the competitive edge.
Hmmm.... I wonder if that's true! Say, how's your water been tasting lately? A little poisony? *You dumb rumor-mongering motherfucker! I poisoned your drinking water!!!*
Holy Fuck!!!

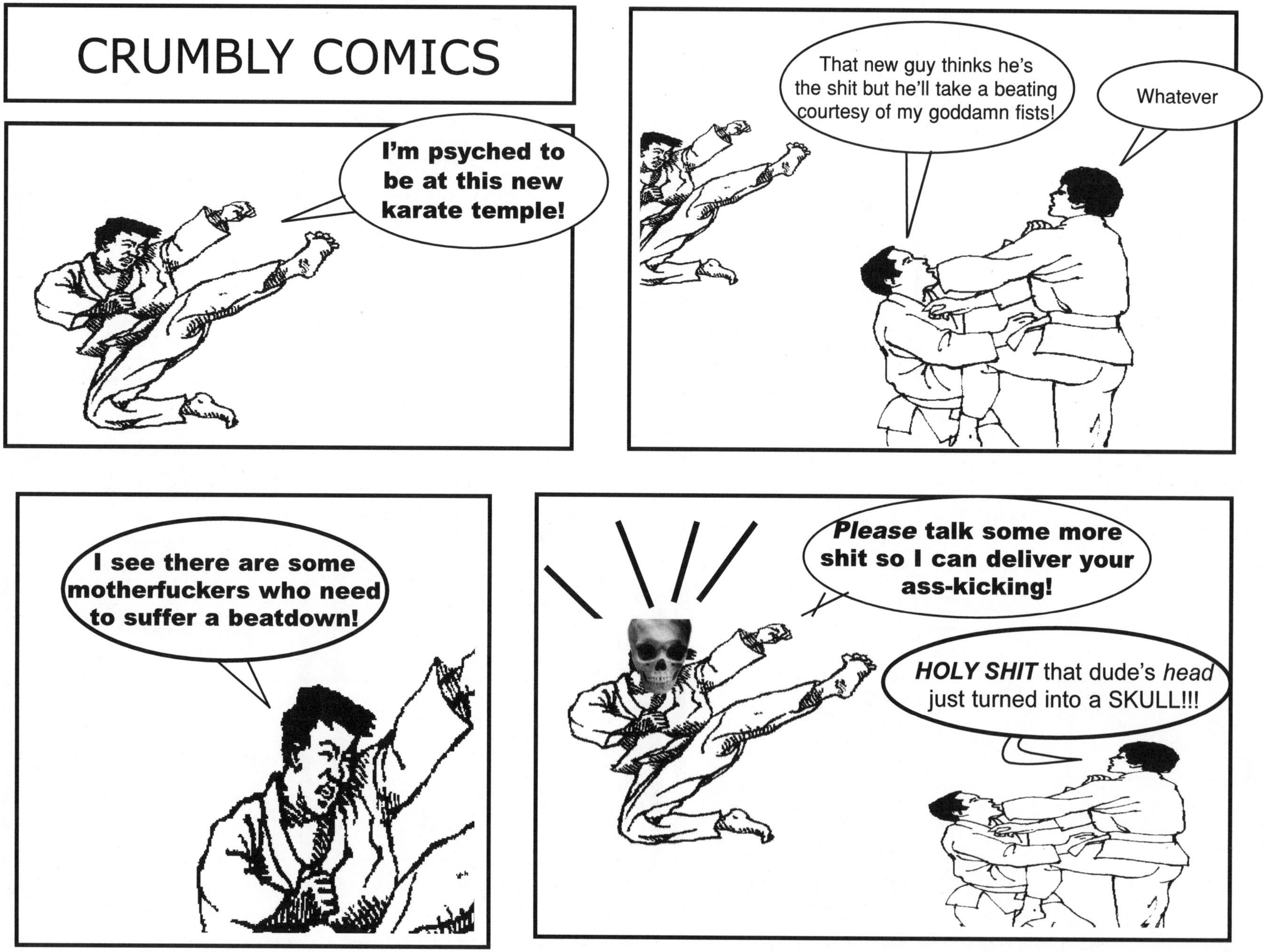
CRUMBLY COMICS
I'm psyched to be at this new karate temple!
That new guy thinks he's the shit but he'll take a beating courtesy of my goddamn fists!
Whatever
I see there are some motherfuckers who need to suffer a beatdown!
Please talk some more shit so I can deliver your ass-kicking!
HOLY SHIT that dude's *head* just turned into a SKULL!!!

"CRUMBLY COMICS"

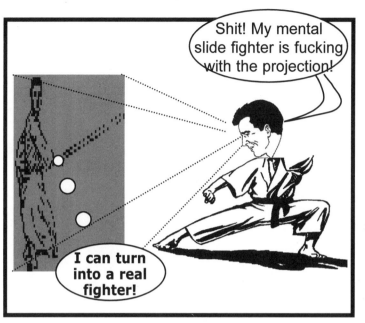

I want to be a real fighter, but I'm a human slide!

I'm gonna break out of this shit!

Shit! My mental slide fighter is fucking with the projection!

I can turn into a real fighter!

HOLY SHIT! I'm so real I have a fucking circulatory system! HOLY FUCK!!!

Goddamn, you look tough as hell!!! Let's team up and fight!

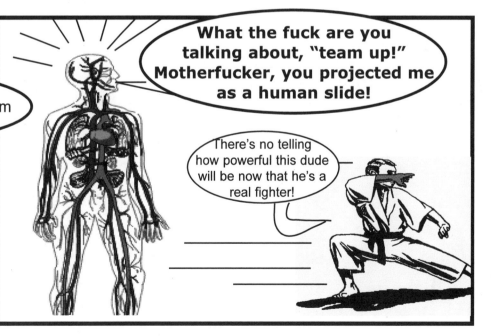

What the fuck are you talking about, "team up!" Motherfucker, you projected me as a human slide!

There's no telling how powerful this dude will be now that he's a real fighter!

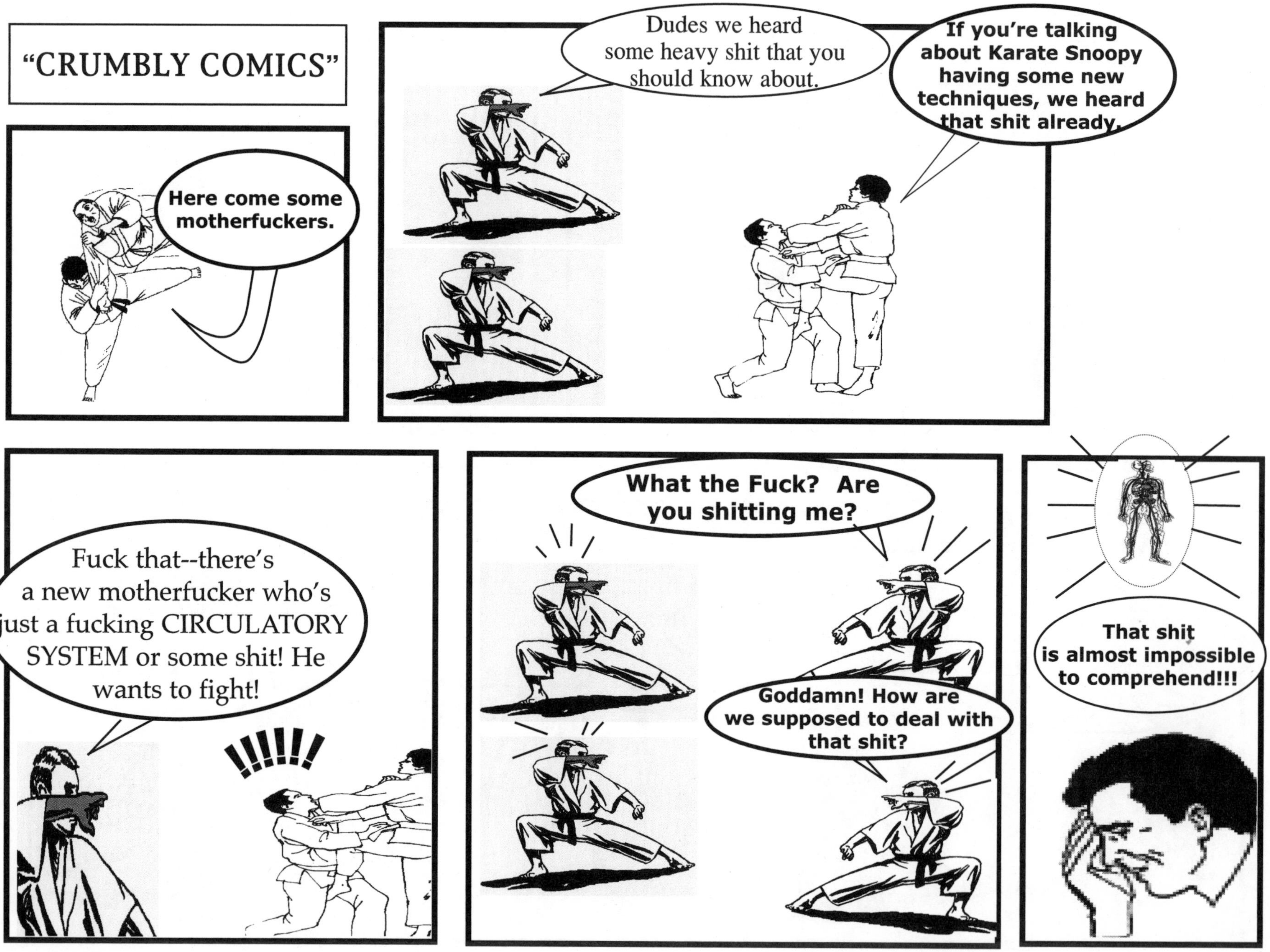
"CRUMBLY COMICS"
Here come some motherfuckers.
Dudes we heard some heavy shit that you should know about.
If you're talking about Karate Snoopy having some new techniques, we heard that shit already.
Fuck that--there's a new motherfucker who's just a fucking CIRCULATORY SYSTEM or some shit! He wants to fight!
!!!!!!
What the Fuck? Are you shitting me?
Goddamn! How are we supposed to deal with that shit?
That shit is almost impossible to comprehend!!!

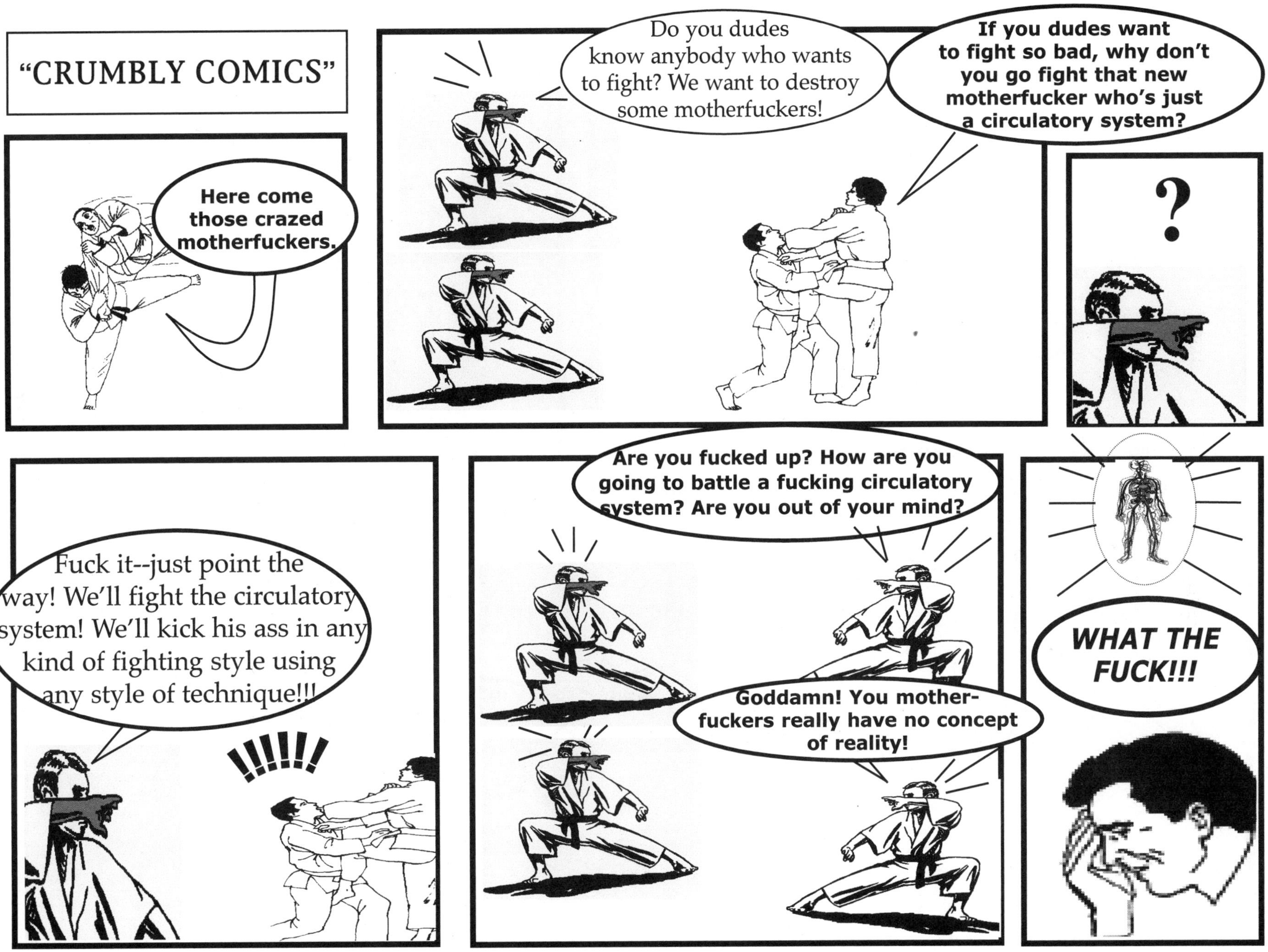
"CRUMBLY COMICS"
Here come those crazed motherfuckers.
Do you dudes know anybody who wants to fight? We want to destroy some motherfuckers!
If you dudes want to fight so bad, why don't you go fight that new motherfucker who's just a circulatory system?
?
Fuck it--just point the way! We'll fight the circulatory system! We'll kick his ass in any kind of fighting style using any style of technique!!!
!!!!!!
Are you fucked up? How are you going to battle a fucking circulatory system? Are you out of your mind?
Goddamn! You mother-fuckers really have no concept of reality!
WHAT THE FUCK!!!

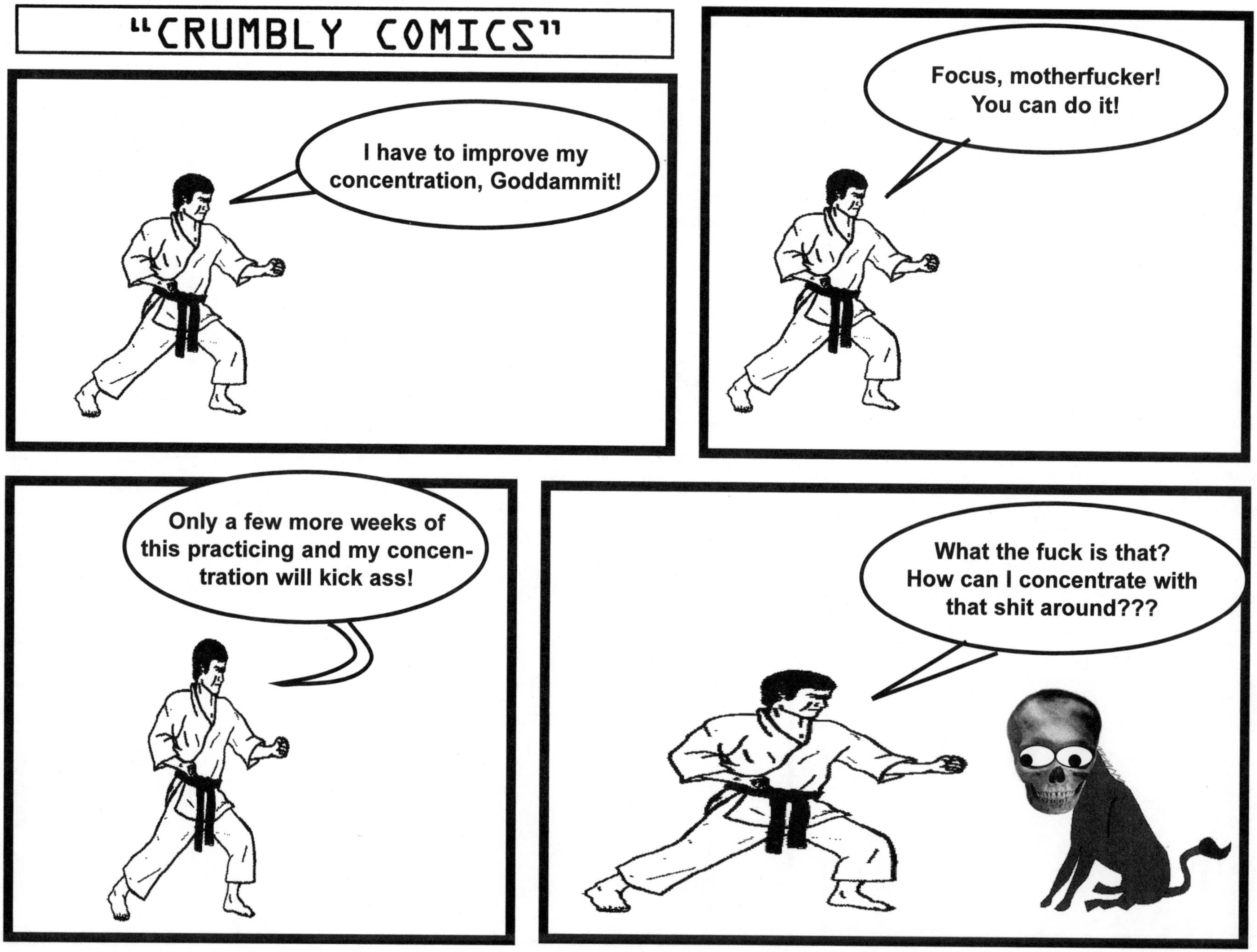
"CRUMBLY COMICS"
I have to improve my concentration, Goddammit!
Focus, motherfucker! You can do it!
Only a few more weeks of this practicing and my concen-tration will kick ass!
What the fuck is that? How can I concentrate with that shit around???

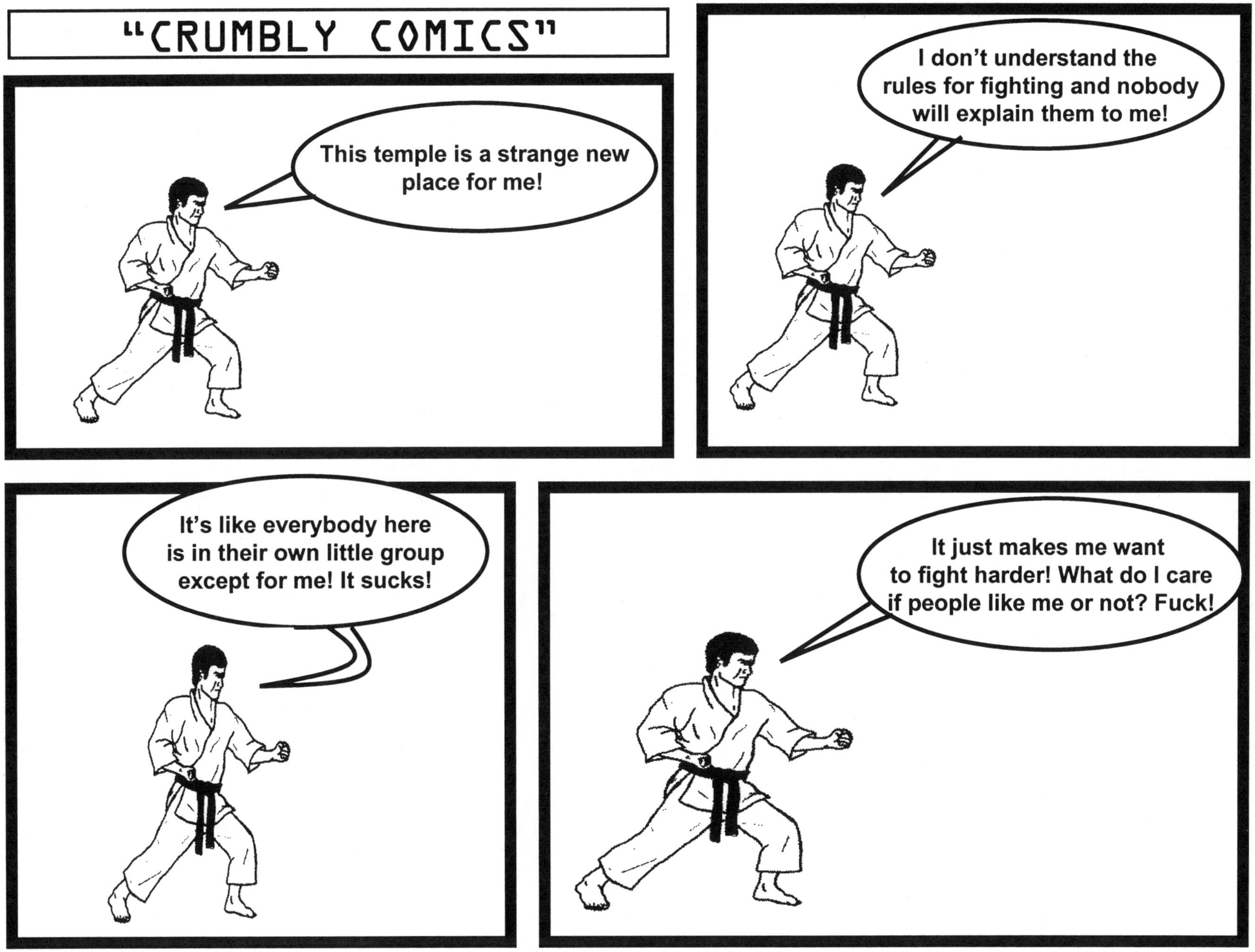
"CRUMBLY COMICS"
This temple is a strange new place for me!
I don't understand the rules for fighting and nobody will explain them to me!
It's like everybody here is in their own little group except for me! It sucks!
It just makes me want to fight harder! What do I care if people like me or not? Fuck!

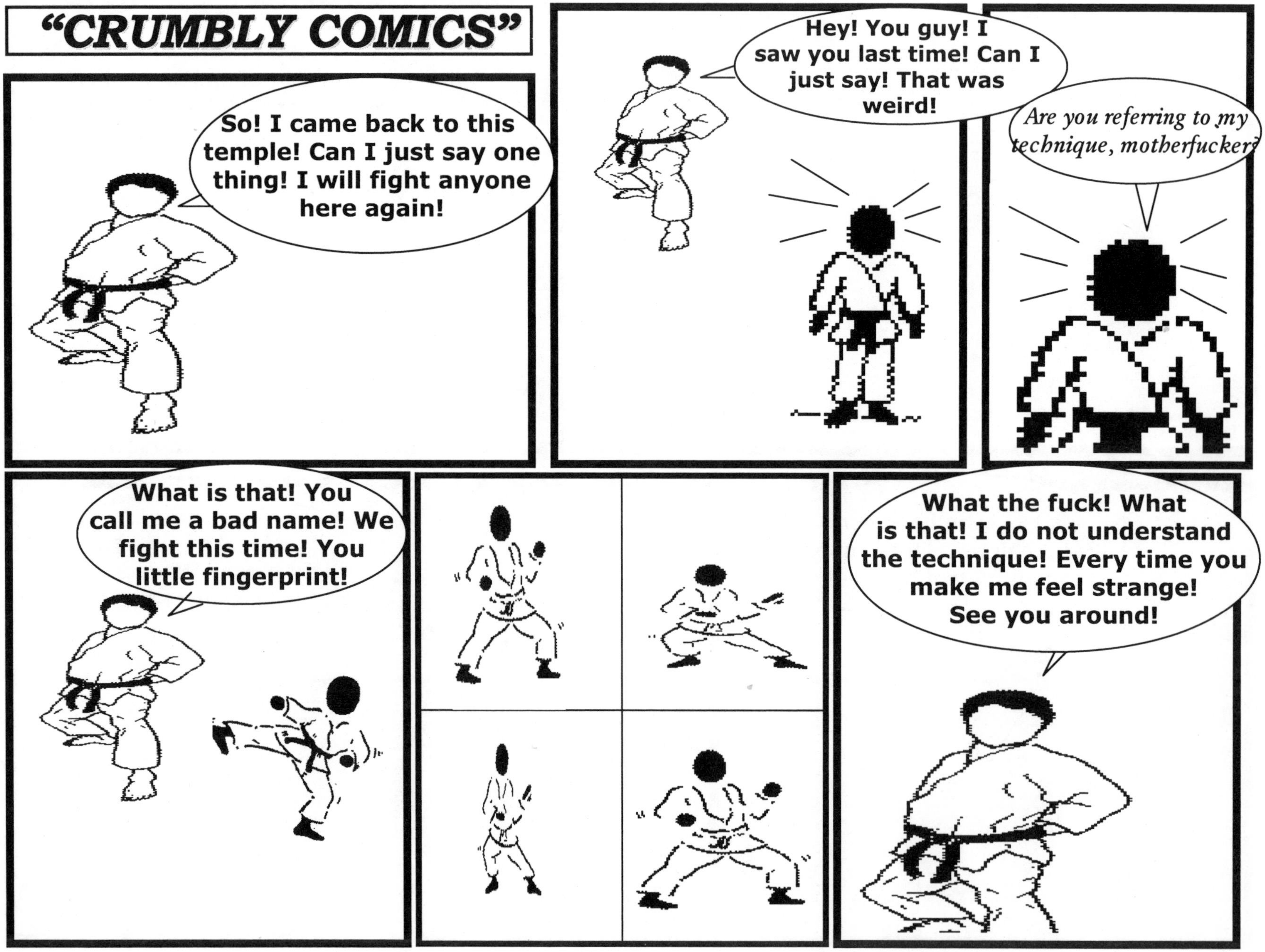
"CRUMBLY COMICS"
So! I came back to this temple! Can I just say one thing! I will fight anyone here again!
Hey! You guy! I saw you last time! Can I just say! That was weird!
Are you referring to my technique, motherfucker?
What is that! You call me a bad name! We fight this time! You little fingerprint!
What the fuck! What is that! I do not understand the technique! Every time you make me feel strange! See you around!

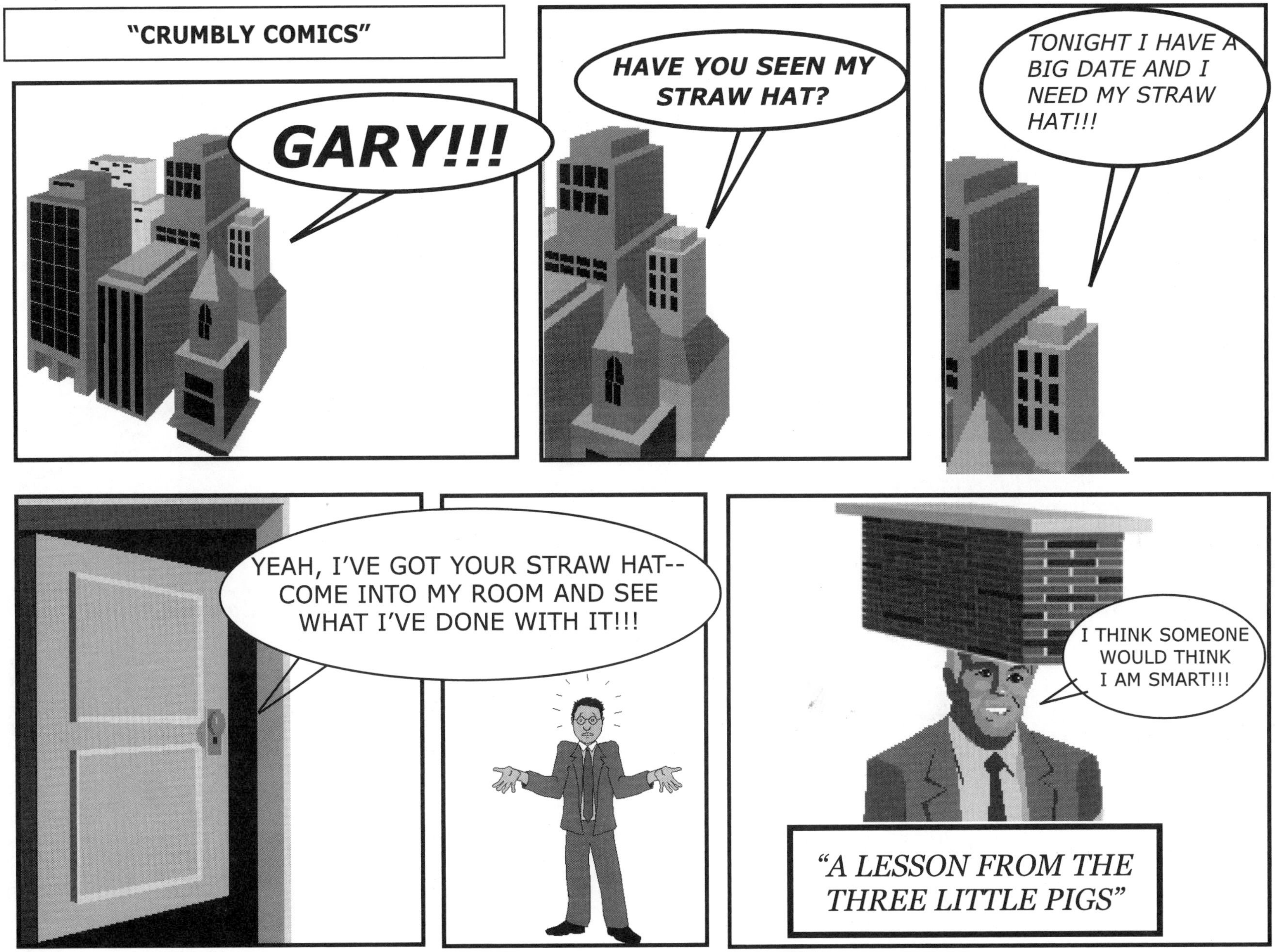
"CRUMBLY COMICS"
GARY!!!
HAVE YOU SEEN MY STRAW HAT?
TONIGHT I HAVE A BIG DATE AND I NEED MY STRAW HAT!!!
YEAH, I'VE GOT YOUR STRAW HAT-- COME INTO MY ROOM AND SEE WHAT I'VE DONE WITH IT!!!
I THINK SOMEONE WOULD THINK I AM SMART!!!
"A LESSON FROM THE THREE LITTLE PIGS"

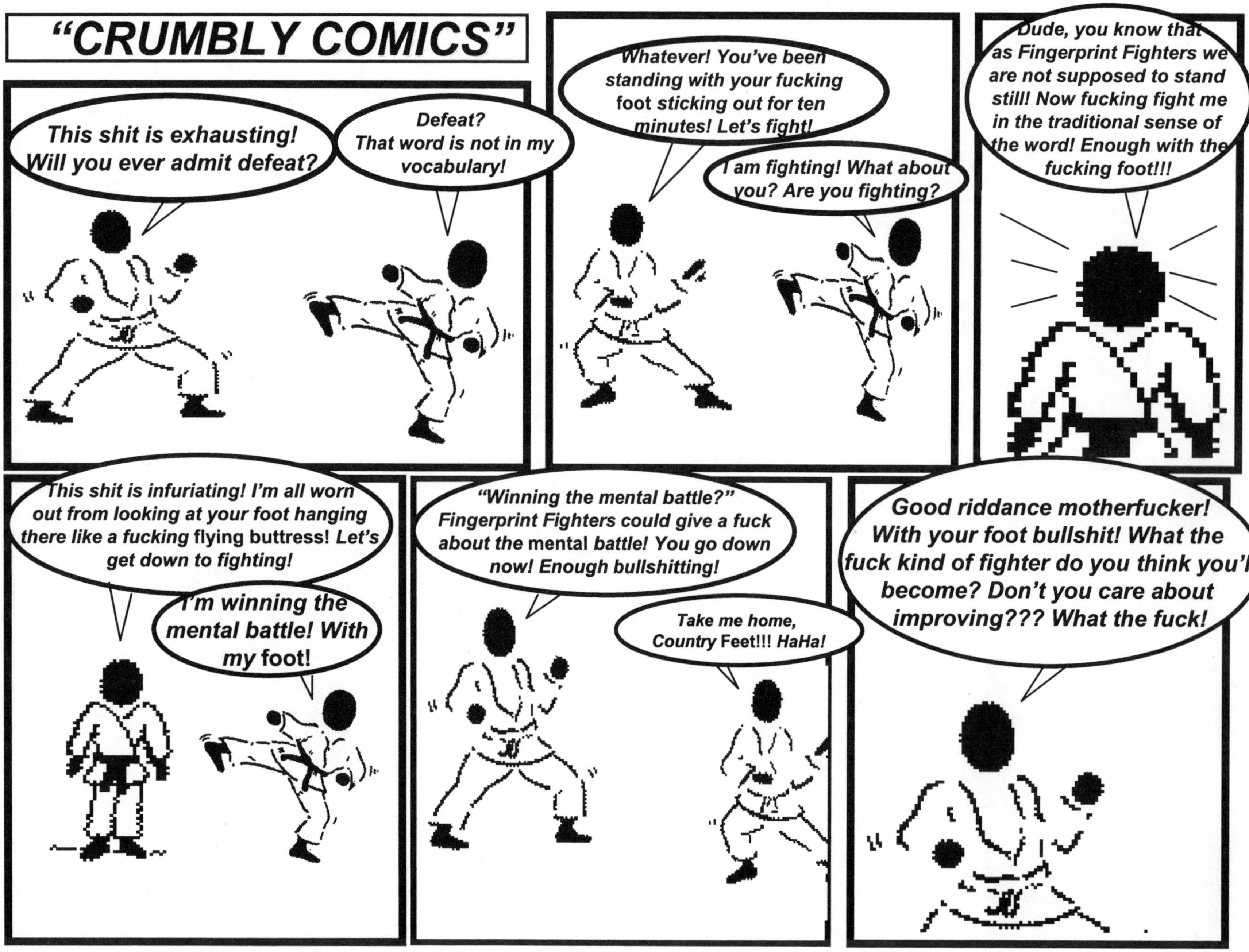

"CRUMBLY COMICS"
This shit is exhausting! Will you ever admit defeat?
Defeat? That word is not in my vocabulary!
Whatever! You've been standing with your fucking foot sticking out for ten minutes! Let's fight!
I am fighting! What about you? Are you fighting?
Dude, you know that as Fingerprint Fighters we are not supposed to stand still! Now fucking fight me in the traditional sense of the word! Enough with the fucking foot!!!
This shit is infuriating! I'm all worn out from looking at your foot hanging there like a fucking flying buttress! Let's get down to fighting!
I'm winning the mental battle! With my foot!
"Winning the mental battle?" Fingerprint Fighters could give a fuck about the mental battle! You go down now! Enough bullshitting!
Take me home, Country Feet!!! HaHa!
Good riddance motherfucker! With your foot bullshit! What the fuck kind of fighter do you think you'll become? Don't you care about improving??? What the fuck!

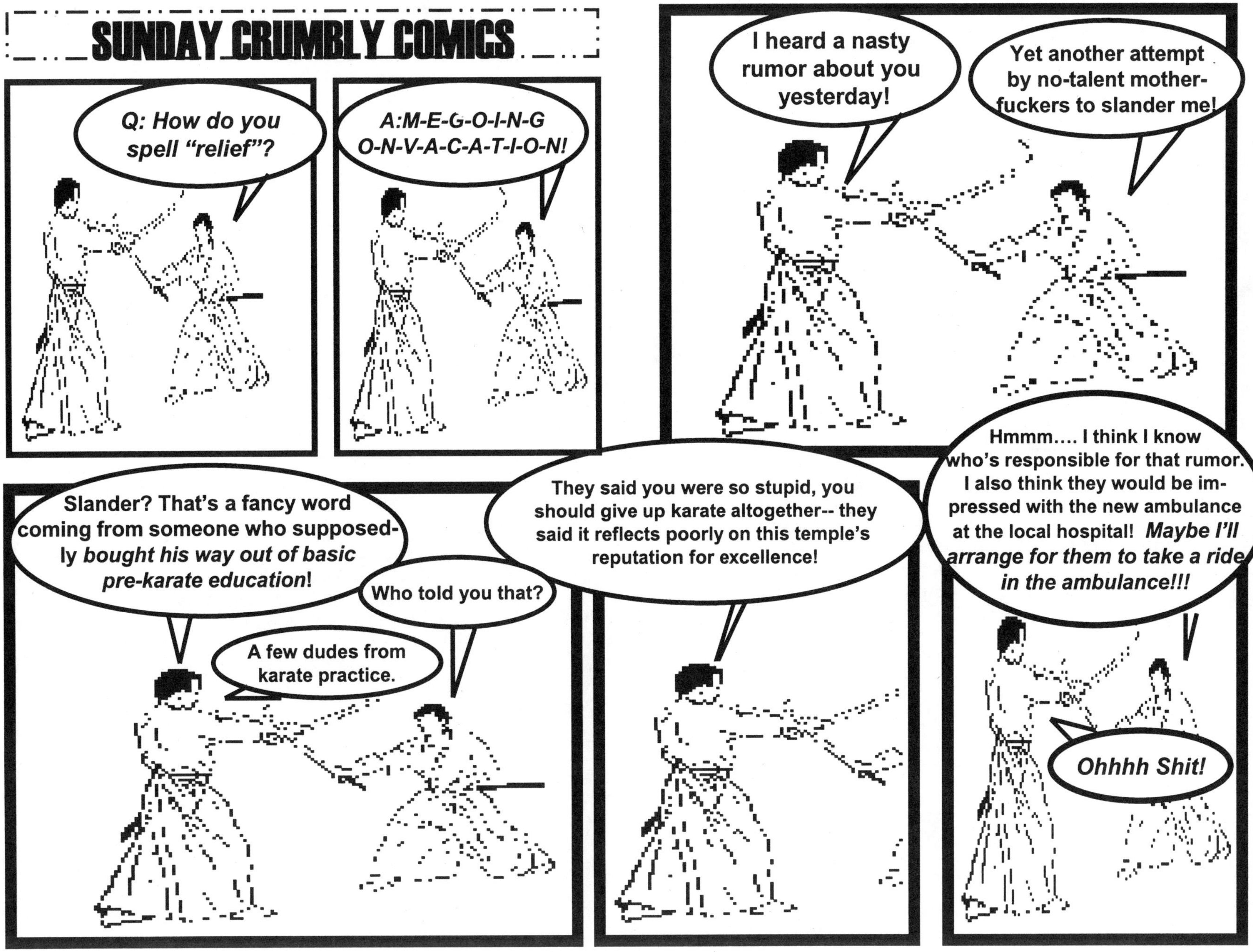
SUNDAY CRUMBLY COMICS
Q: How do you spell "relief"?
A:M-E-G-O-I-N-G O-N-V-A-C-A-T-I-O-N!
I heard a nasty rumor about you yesterday!
Yet another attempt by no-talent mother-fuckers to slander me!
Slander? That's a fancy word coming from someone who supposed-ly *bought his way out of basic pre-karate education*!
Who told you that?
A few dudes from karate practice.
They said you were so stupid, you should give up karate altogether-- they said it reflects poorly on this temple's reputation for excellence!
Hmmm.... I think I know who's responsible for that rumor. I also think they would be im-pressed with the new ambulance at the local hospital! *Maybe I'll arrange for them to take a ride in the ambulance!!!*
Ohhhh Shit!

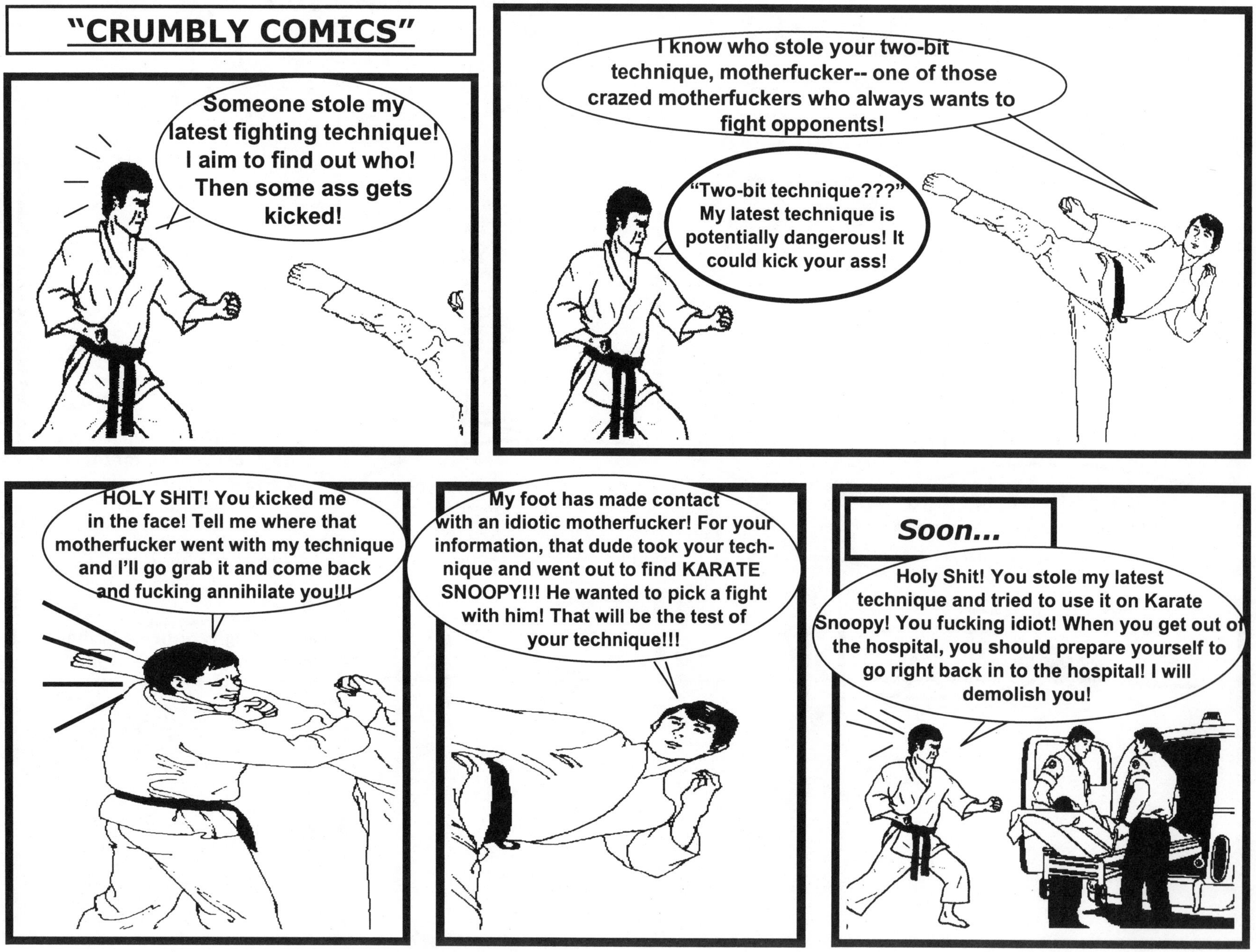
"CRUMBLY COMICS"
Someone stole my latest fighting technique! I aim to find out who! Then some ass gets kicked!
I know who stole your two-bit technique, motherfucker-- one of those crazed motherfuckers who always wants to fight opponents!
"Two-bit technique???" My latest technique is potentially dangerous! It could kick your ass!
HOLY SHIT! You kicked me in the face! Tell me where that motherfucker went with my technique and I'll go grab it and come back and fucking annihilate you!!!
My foot has made contact with an idiotic motherfucker! For your information, that dude took your tech-nique and went out to find KARATE SNOOPY!!! He wanted to pick a fight with him! That will be the test of your technique!!!
Soon...
Holy Shit! You stole my latest technique and tried to use it on Karate Snoopy! You fucking idiot! When you get out of the hospital, you should prepare yourself to go right back in to the hospital! I will demolish you!

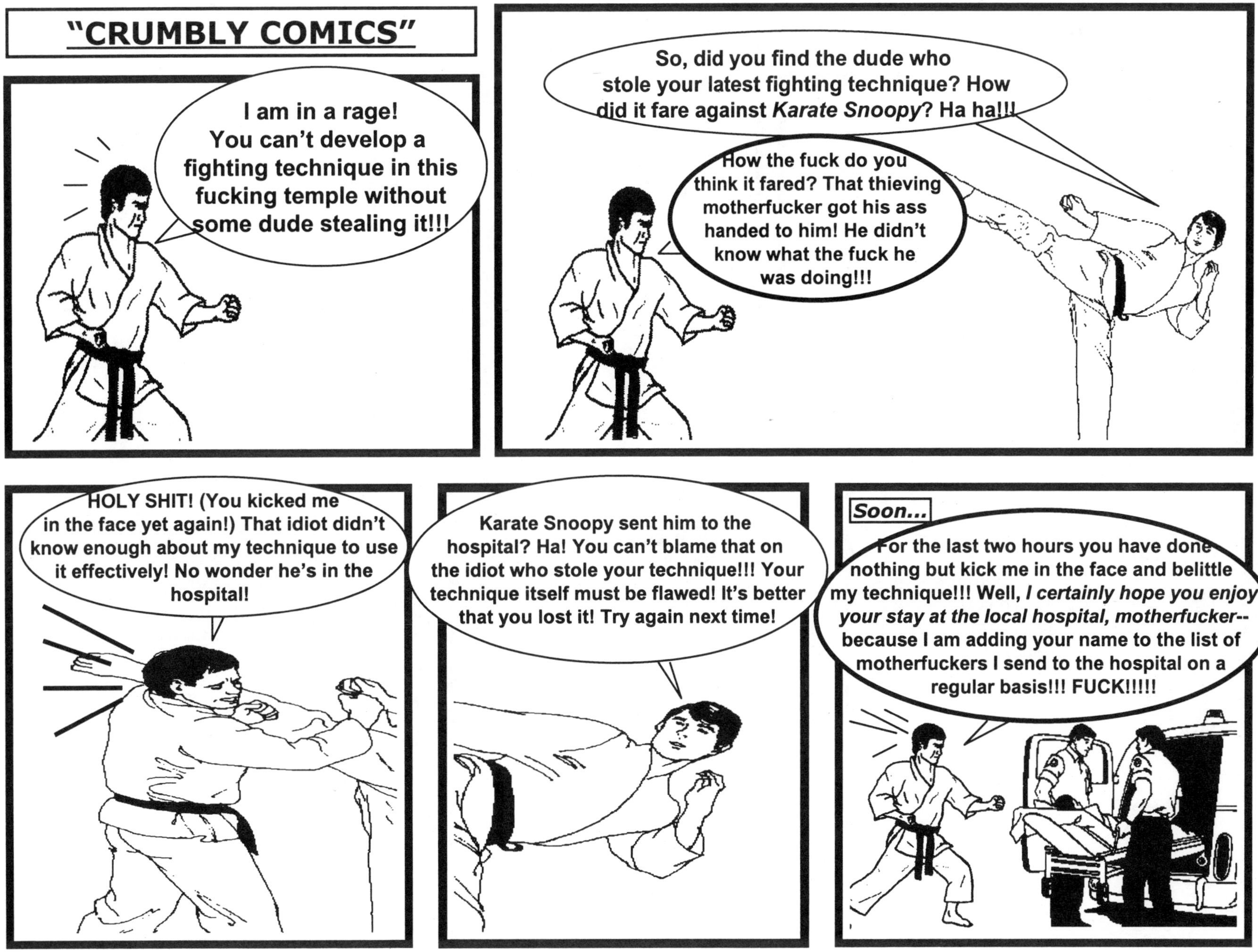
"CRUMBLY COMICS"
I am in a rage! You can't develop a fighting technique in this fucking temple without some dude stealing it!!!
So, did you find the dude who stole your latest fighting technique? How did it fare against *Karate Snoopy*? Ha ha!!!
How the fuck do you think it fared? That thieving motherfucker got his ass handed to him! He didn't know what the fuck he was doing!!!
HOLY SHIT! (You kicked me in the face yet again!) That idiot didn't know enough about my technique to use it effectively! No wonder he's in the hospital!
Karate Snoopy sent him to the hospital? Ha! You can't blame that on the idiot who stole your technique!!! Your technique itself must be flawed! It's better that you lost it! Try again next time!
Soon...
For the last two hours you have done nothing but kick me in the face and belittle my technique!!! Well, *I certainly hope you enjoy your stay at the local hospital, motherfucker*--because I am adding your name to the list of motherfuckers I send to the hospital on a regular basis!!! FUCK!!!!!

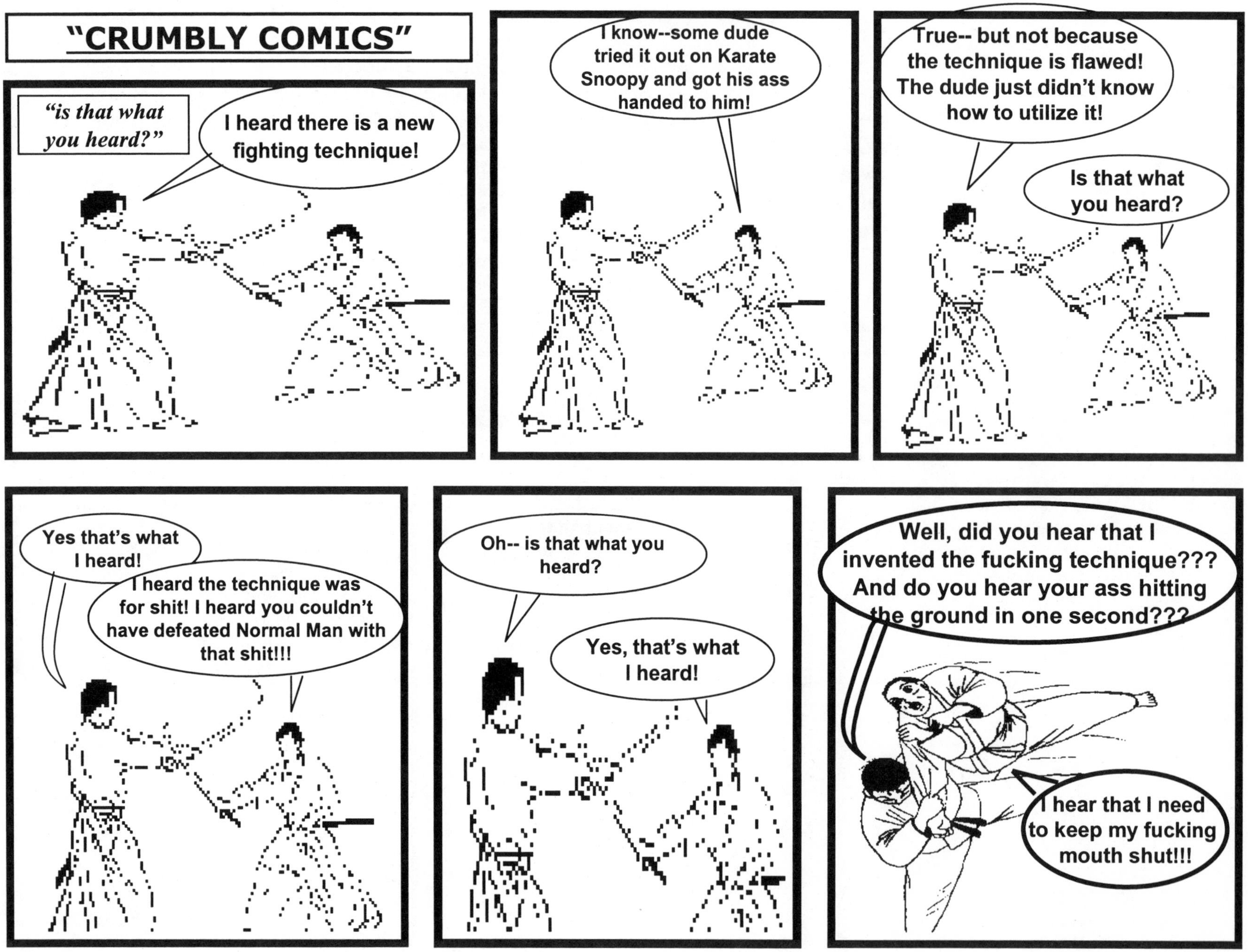
"CRUMBLY COMICS"
"is that what you heard?"
I heard there is a new fighting technique!
I know--some dude tried it out on Karate Snoopy and got his ass handed to him!
True-- but not because the technique is flawed! The dude just didn't know how to utilize it!
Is that what you heard?
Yes that's what I heard!
I heard the technique was for shit! I heard you couldn't have defeated Normal Man with that shit!!!
Oh-- is that what you heard?
Yes, that's what I heard!
Well, did you hear that I invented the fucking technique??? And do you hear your ass hitting the ground in one second???
I hear that I need to keep my fucking mouth shut!!!

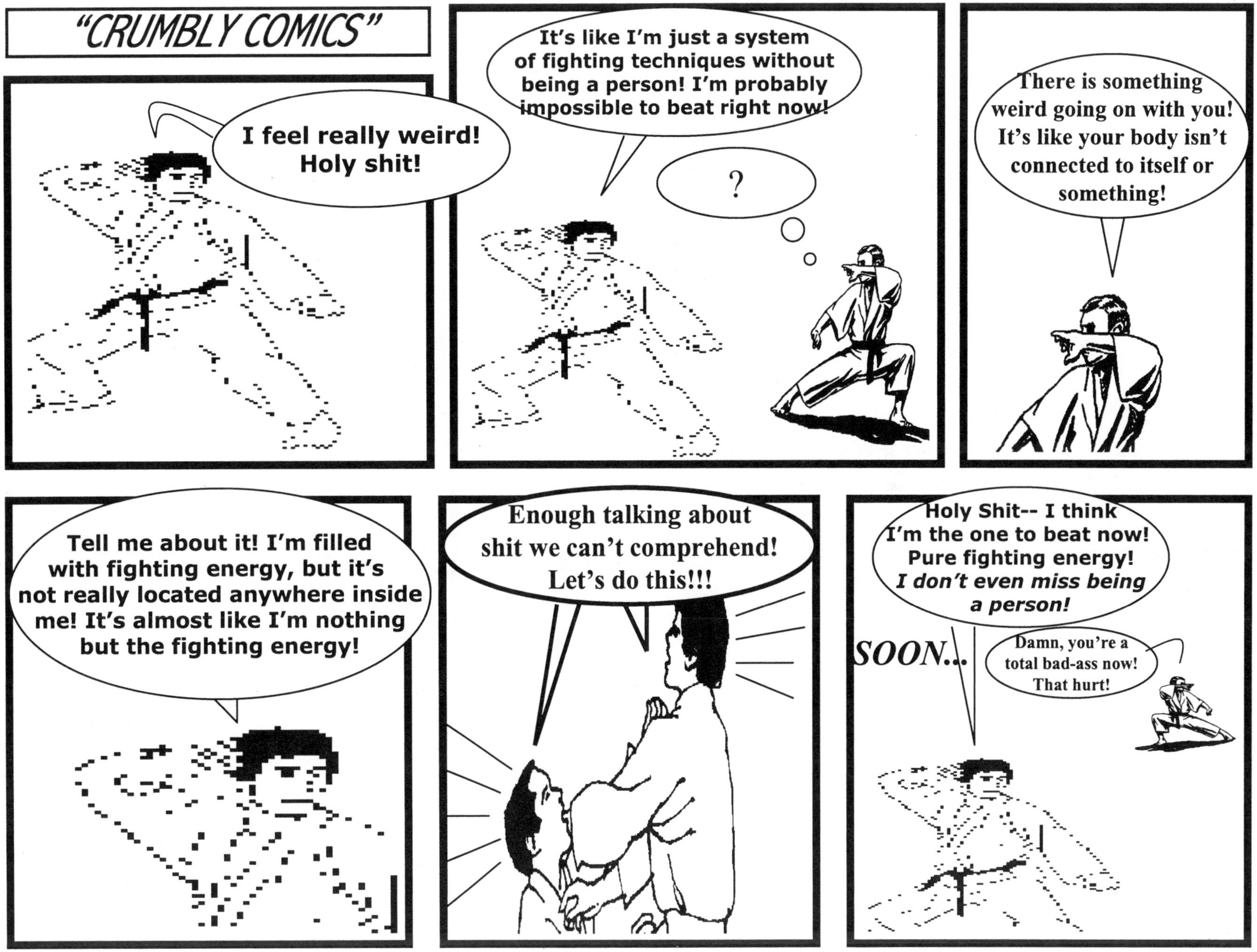
"CRUMBLY COMICS"
I feel really weird! Holy shit!
It's like I'm just a system of fighting techniques without being a person! I'm probably impossible to beat right now!
?
There is something weird going on with you! It's like your body isn't connected to itself or something!
Tell me about it! I'm filled with fighting energy, but it's not really located anywhere inside me! It's almost like I'm nothing but the fighting energy!
Enough talking about shit we can't comprehend! Let's do this!!!
SOON...
Holy Shit-- I think I'm the one to beat now! Pure fighting energy! *I don't even miss being a person!*
Damn, you're a total bad-ass now! That hurt!

"CRUMBLY COMICS"

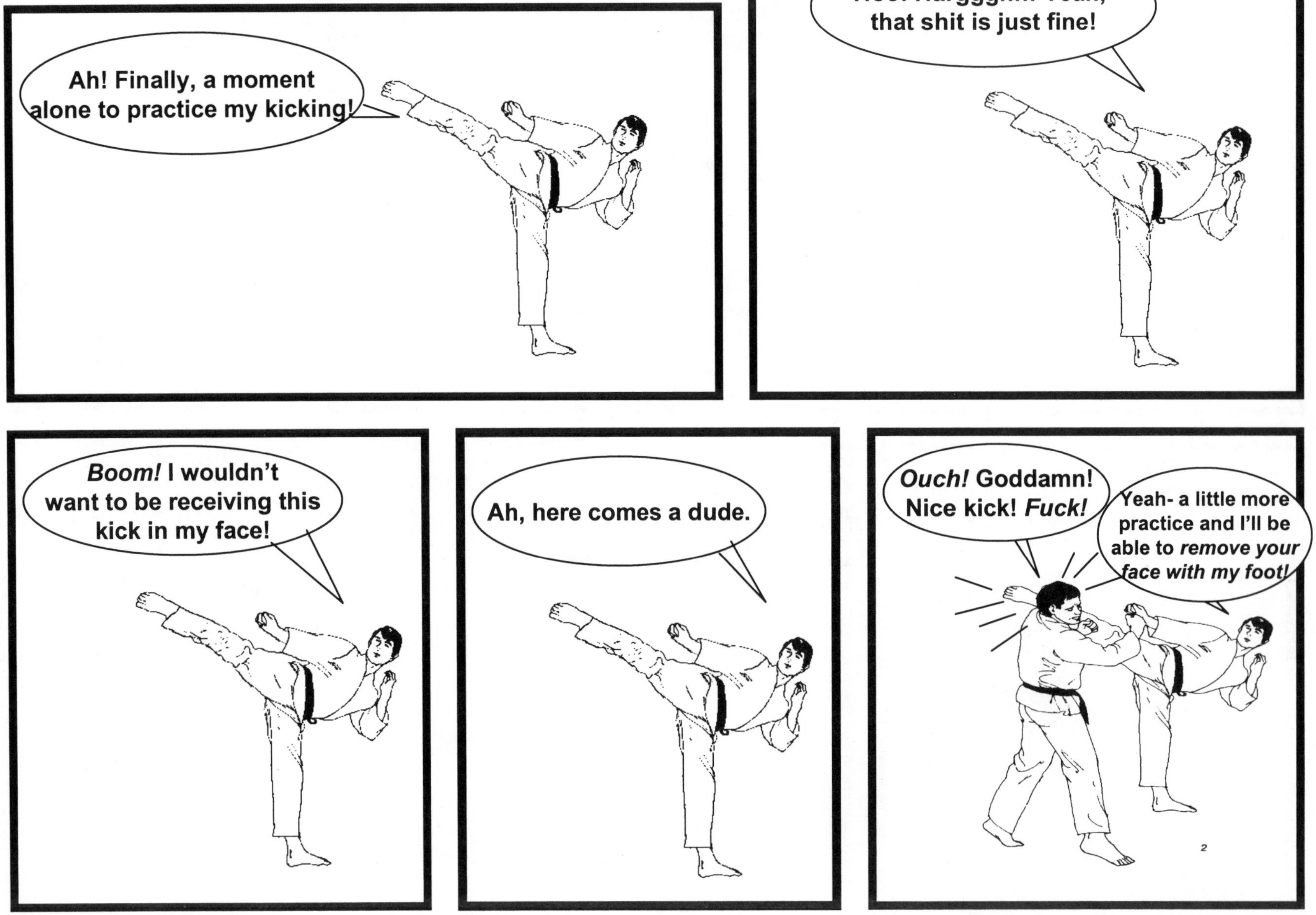

Ah! Finally, a moment alone to practice my kicking!
Hoo! Harggghh! Yeah, that shit is just fine!
Boom! I wouldn't want to be receiving this kick in my face!
Ah, here comes a dude.
Ouch! Goddamn! Nice kick! *Fuck!*
Yeah- a little more practice and I'll be able to *remove your face with my foot!*

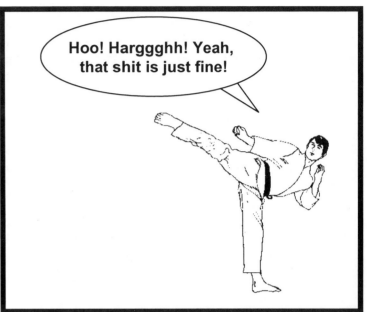

"CRUMBLER COMICS"

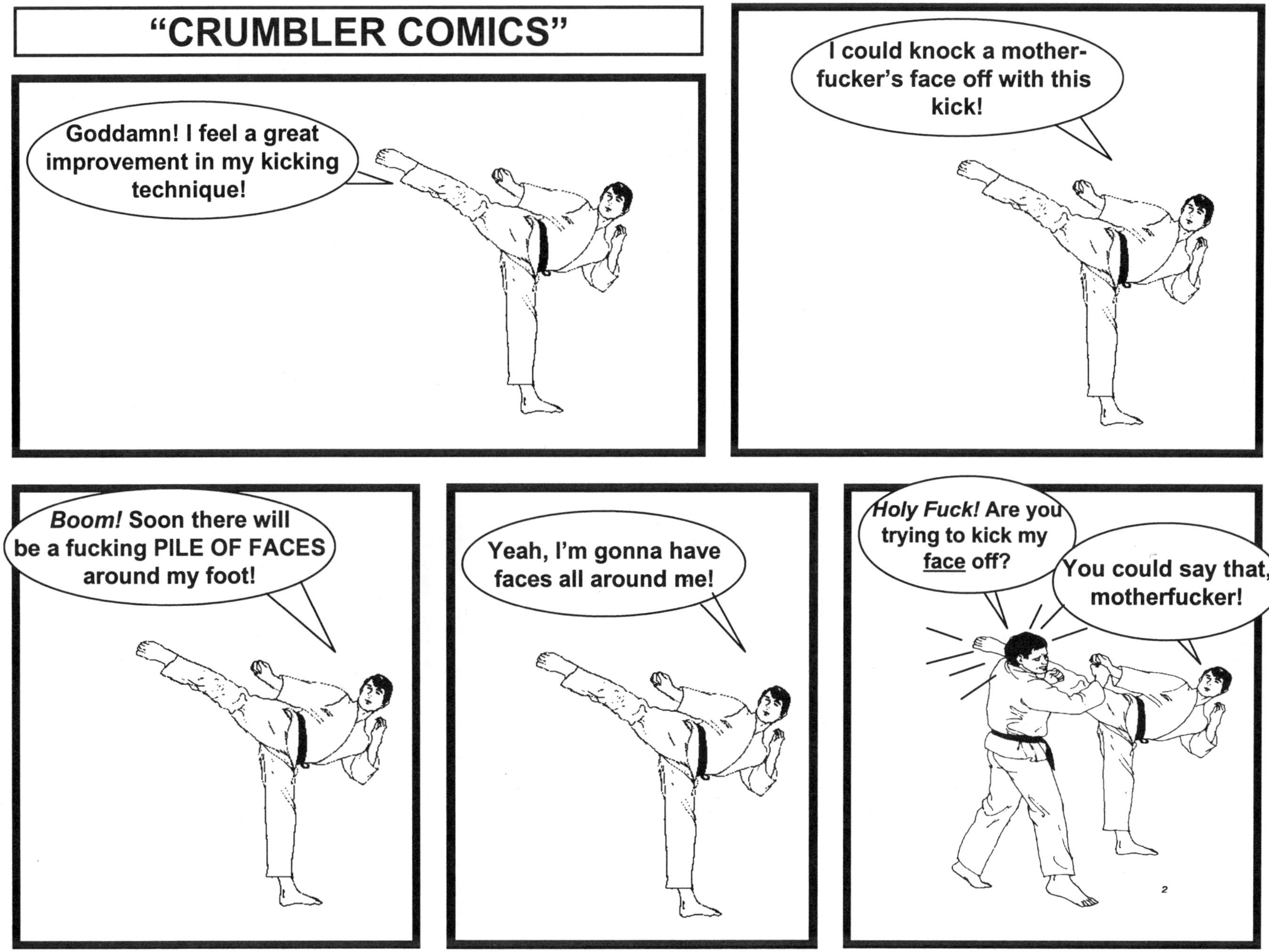

Goddamn! I feel a great improvement in my kicking technique!
I could knock a mother-fucker's face off with this kick!
Boom! Soon there will be a fucking PILE OF FACES around my foot!
Yeah, I'm gonna have faces all around me!
Holy Fuck! Are you trying to kick my face off?
You could say that, motherfucker!

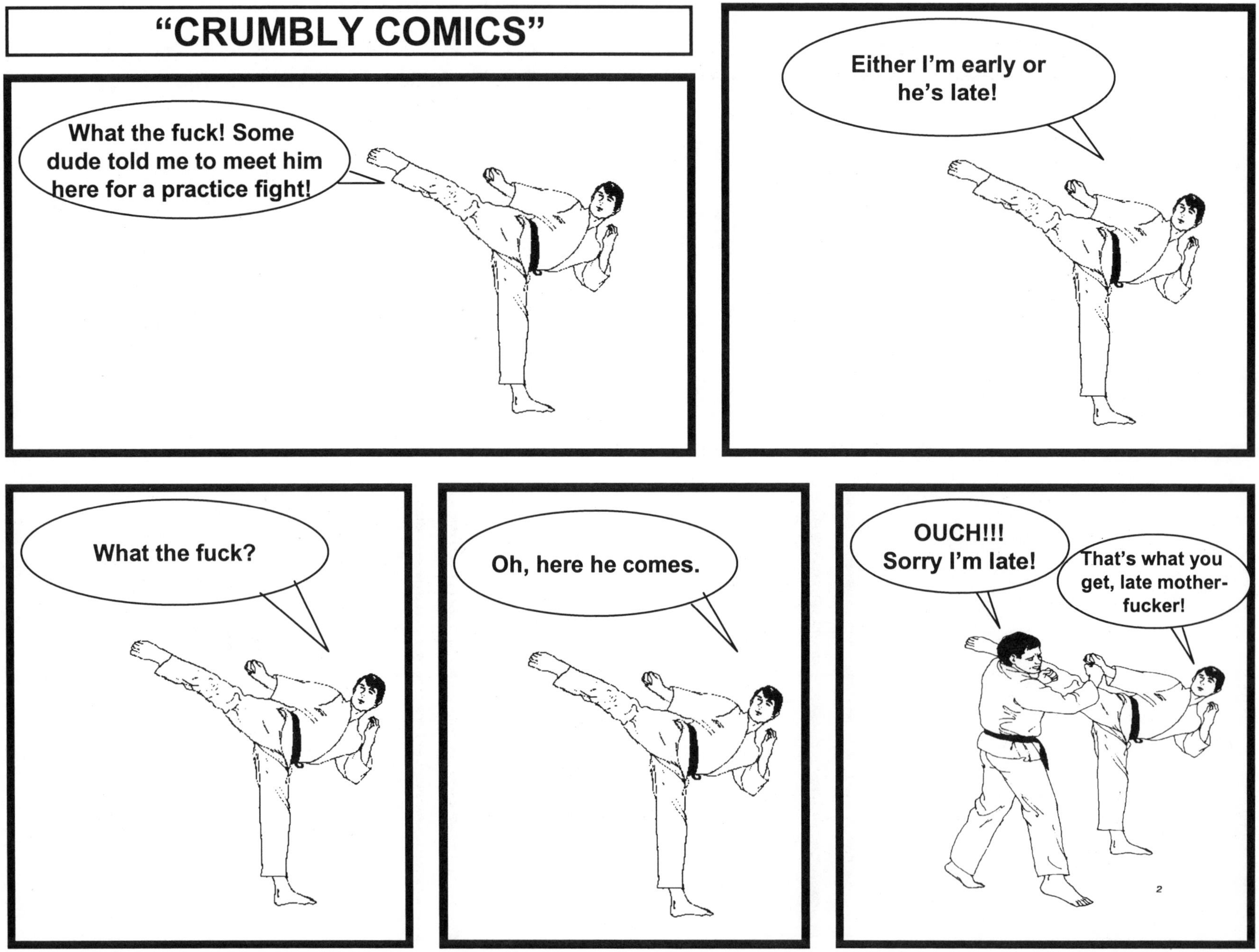
"CRUMBLY COMICS"
What the fuck! Some dude told me to meet him here for a practice fight!
Either I'm early or he's late!
What the fuck?
Oh, here he comes.
OUCH!!! Sorry I'm late!
That's what you get, late mother-fucker!
2

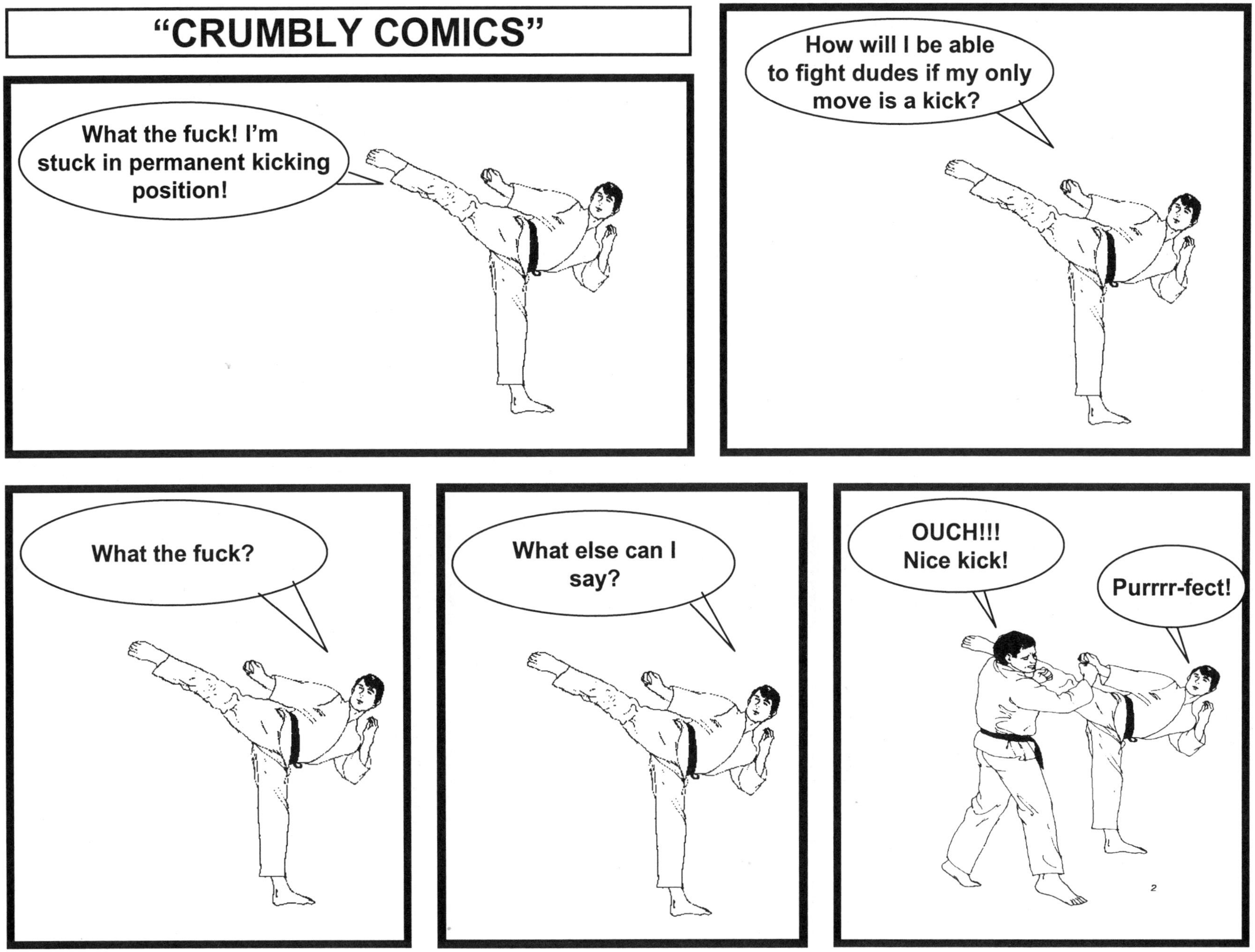
"CRUMBLY COMICS"
What the fuck! I'm stuck in permanent kicking position!
How will I be able to fight dudes if my only move is a kick?
What the fuck?
What else can I say?
OUCH!!! Nice kick!
Purrrr-fect!
2

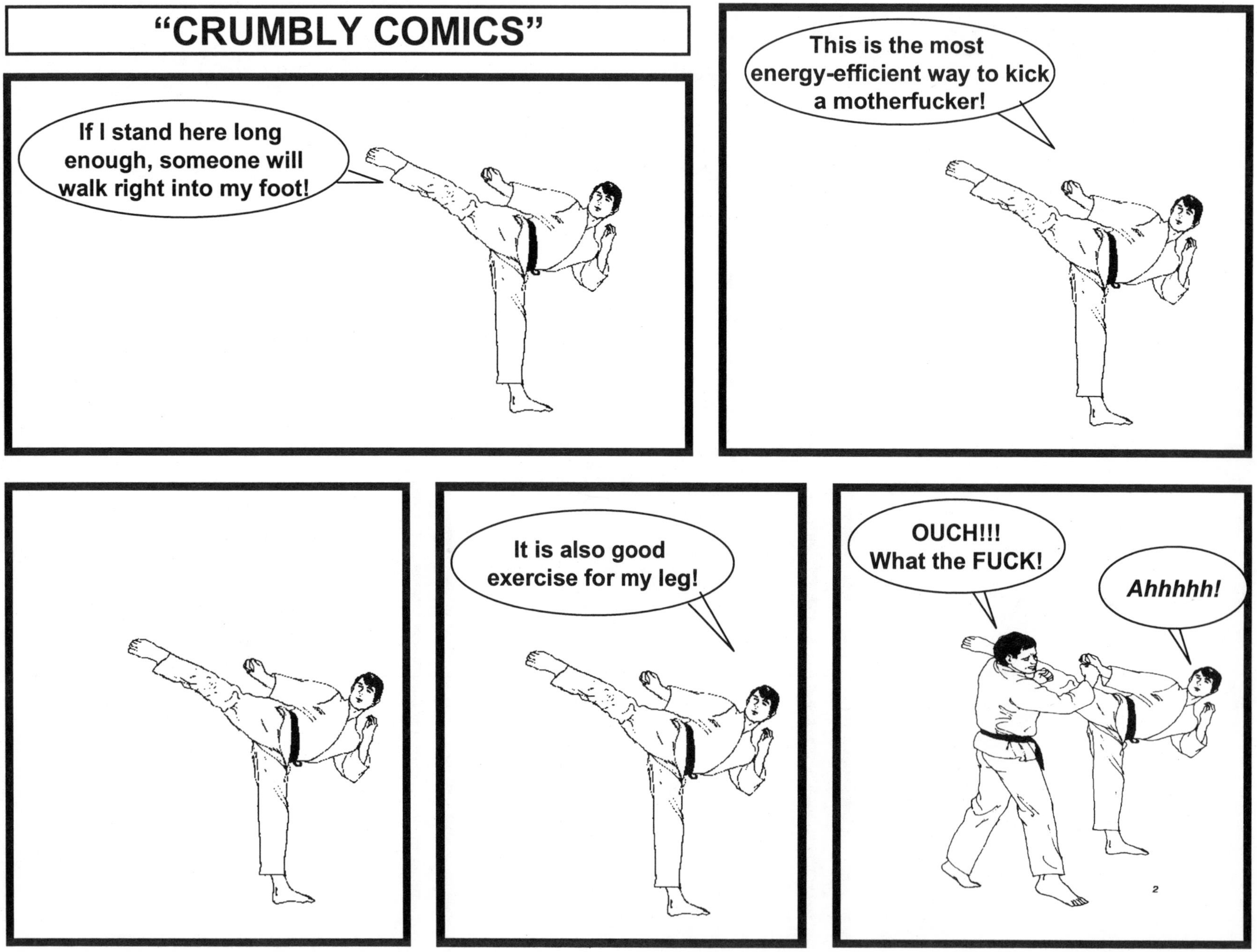
"CRUMBLY COMICS"
If I stand here long enough, someone will walk right into my foot!
This is the most energy-efficient way to kick a motherfucker!
It is also good exercise for my leg!
OUCH!!! What the FUCK!
Ahhhhh!

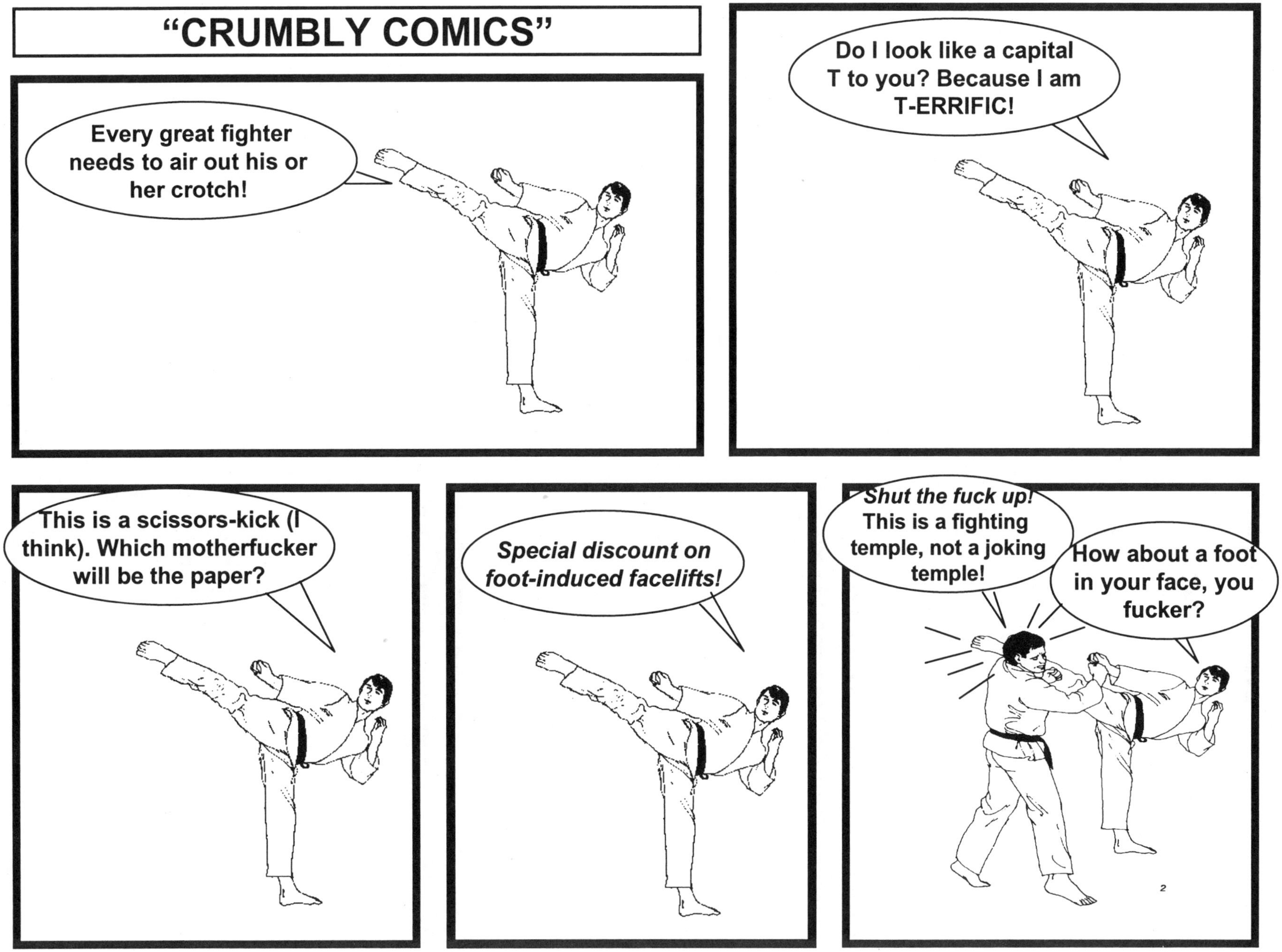
"CRUMBLY COMICS"
Every great fighter needs to air out his or her crotch!
Do I look like a capital T to you? Because I am T-ERRIFIC!
This is a scissors-kick (I think). Which motherfucker will be the paper?
Special discount on foot-induced facelifts!
Shut the fuck up! This is a fighting temple, not a joking temple!
How about a foot in your face, you fucker?

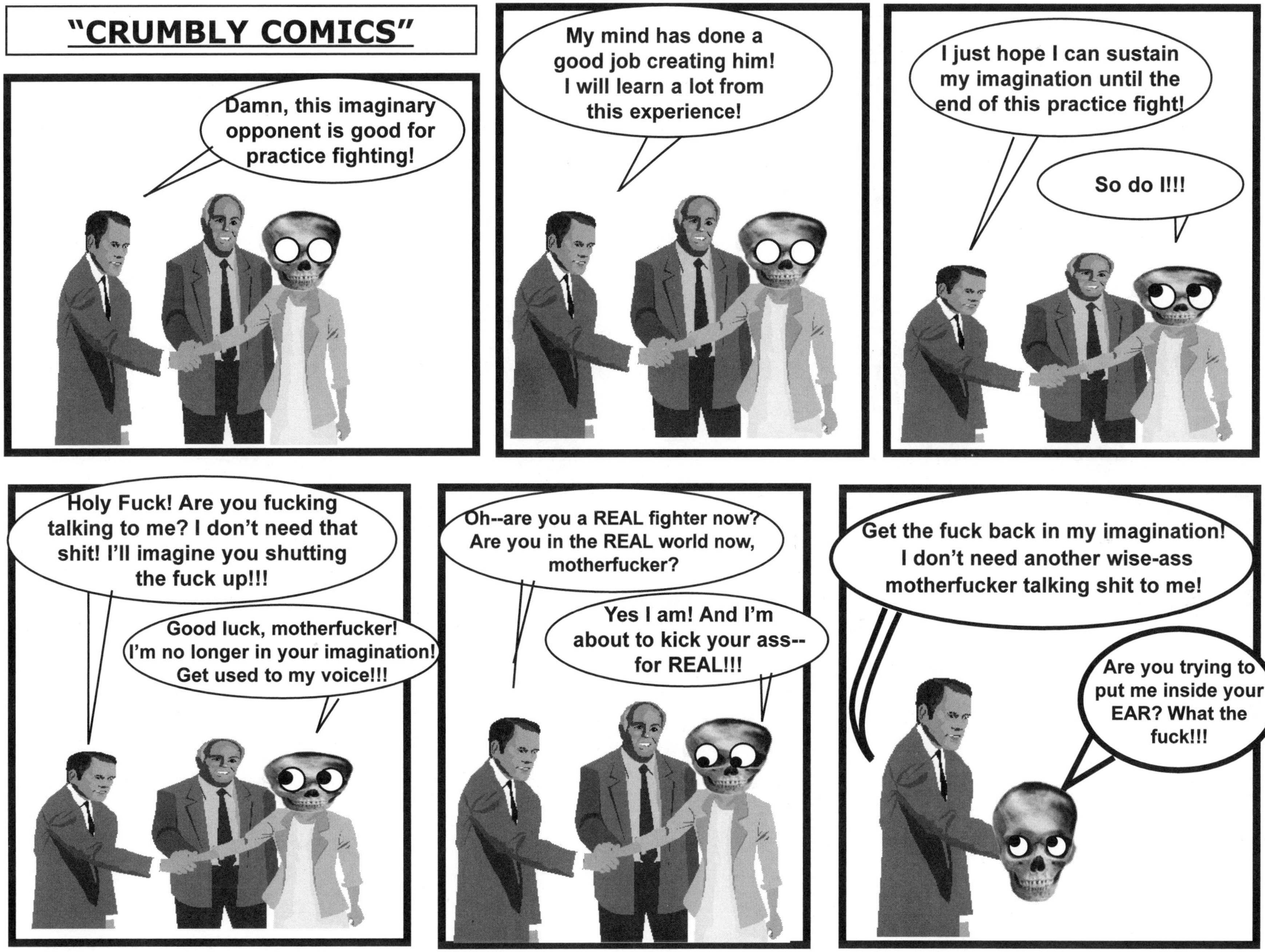
"CRUMBLY COMICS"
Damn, this imaginary opponent is good for practice fighting!
My mind has done a good job creating him! I will learn a lot from this experience!
I just hope I can sustain my imagination until the end of this practice fight!
So do I!!!
Holy Fuck! Are you fucking talking to me? I don't need that shit! I'll imagine you shutting the fuck up!!!
Good luck, motherfucker! I'm no longer in your imagination! Get used to my voice!!!
Oh--are you a REAL fighter now? Are you in the REAL world now, motherfucker?
Yes I am! And I'm about to kick your ass--for REAL!!!
Get the fuck back in my imagination! I don't need another wise-ass motherfucker talking shit to me!
Are you trying to put me inside your EAR? What the fuck!!!

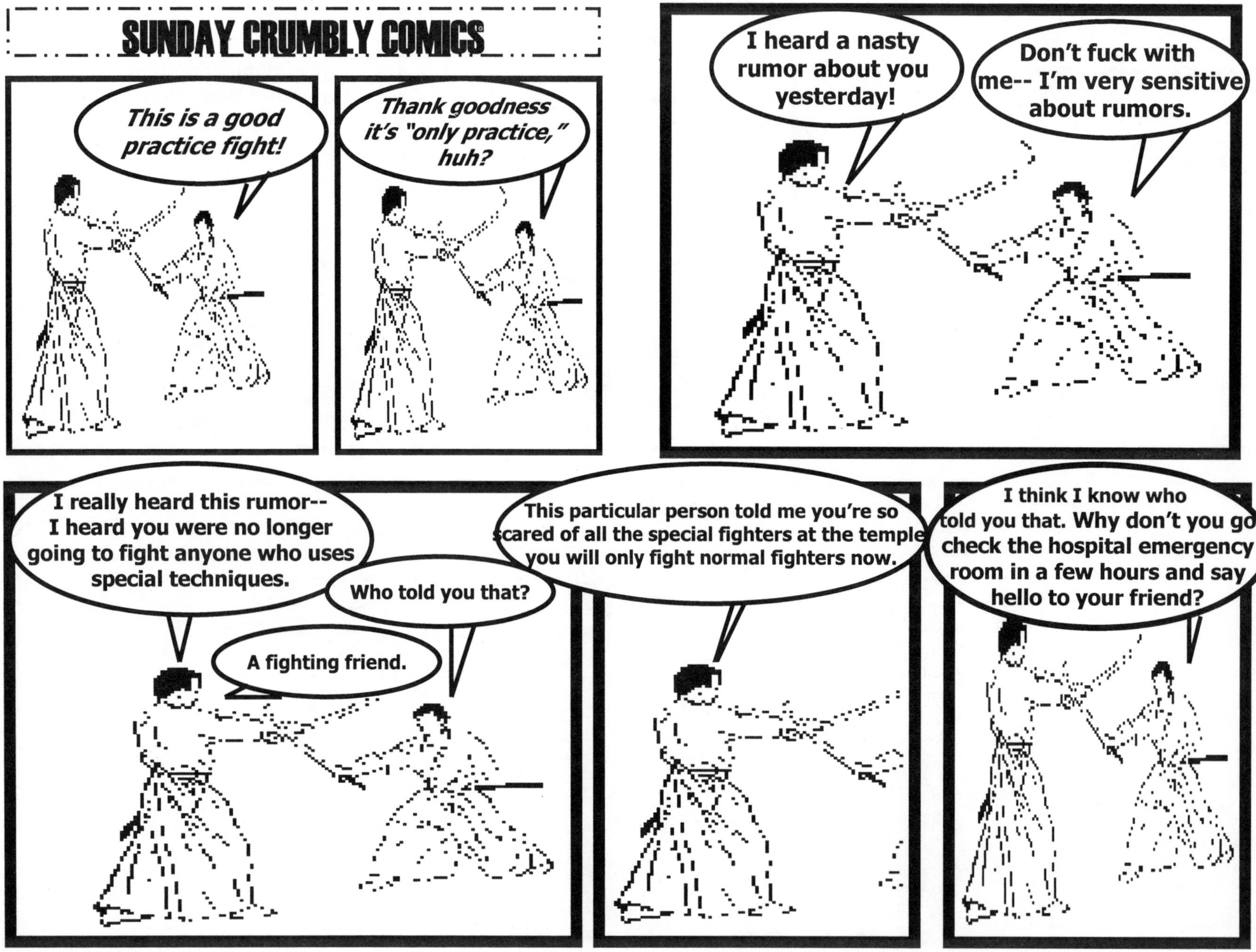
SUNDAY CRUMBLY COMICS
This is a good practice fight!
Thank goodness it's "only practice," huh?
I heard a nasty rumor about you yesterday!
Don't fuck with me-- I'm very sensitive about rumors.
I really heard this rumor-- I heard you were no longer going to fight anyone who uses special techniques.
Who told you that?
A fighting friend.
This particular person told me you're so scared of all the special fighters at the temple you will only fight normal fighters now.
I think I know who told you that. Why don't you go check the hospital emergency room in a few hours and say hello to your friend?

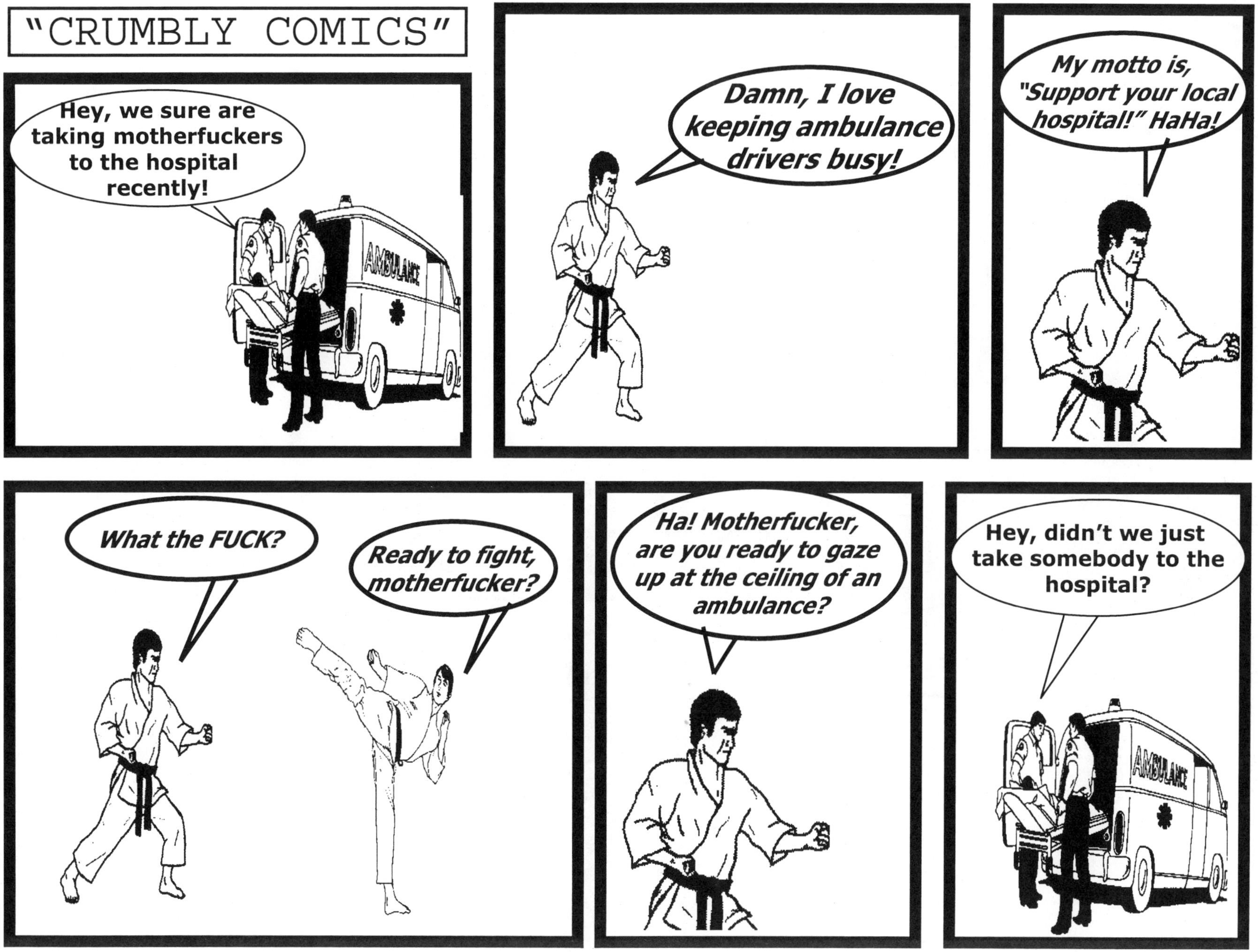
"CRUMBLY COMICS"
Hey, we sure are taking motherfuckers to the hospital recently!
AMBULANCE
Damn, I love keeping ambulance drivers busy!
My motto is, "Support your local hospital!" HaHa!
What the FUCK?
Ready to fight, motherfucker?
Ha! Motherfucker, are you ready to gaze up at the ceiling of an ambulance?
Hey, didn't we just take somebody to the hospital?
AMBULANCE

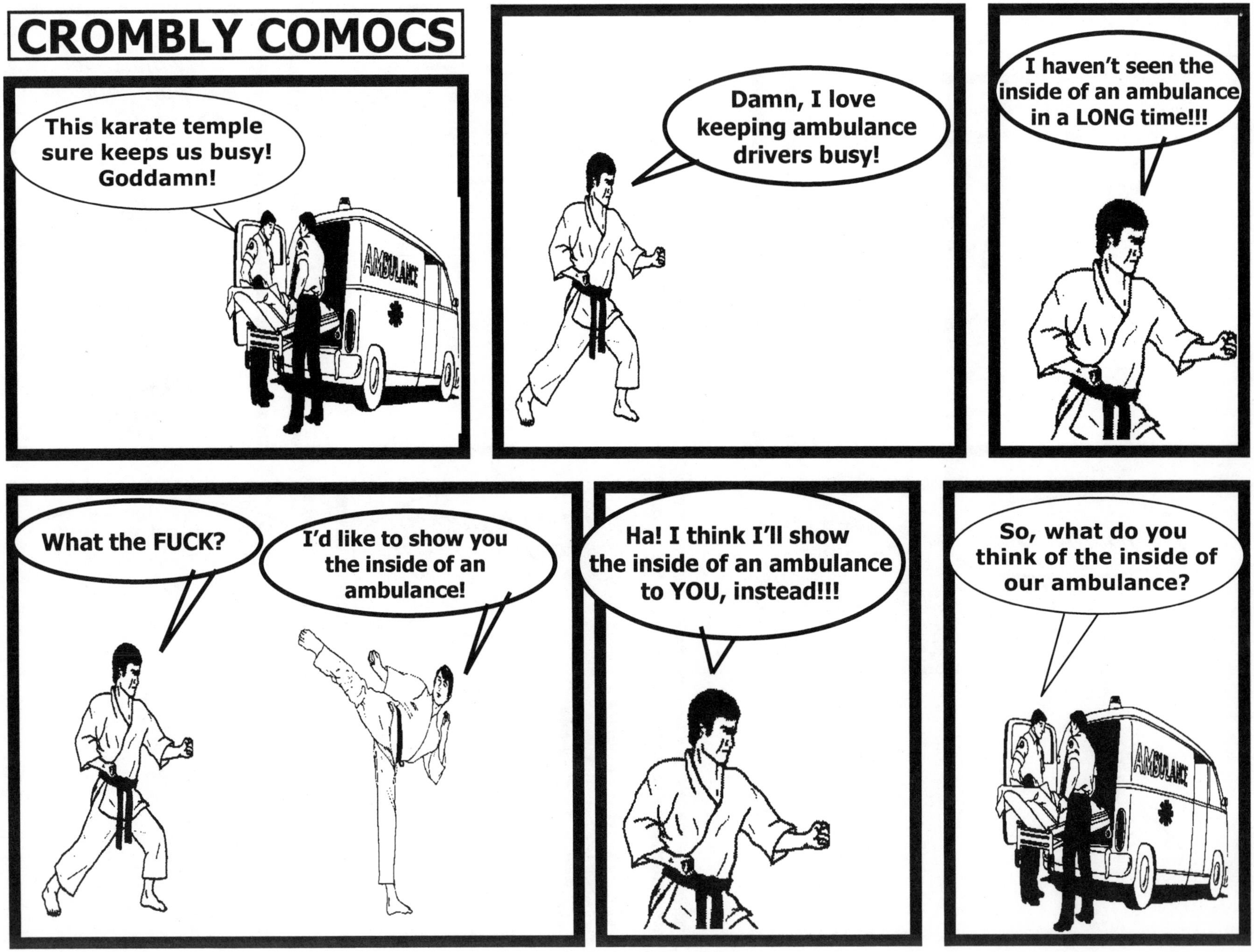
CROMBLY COMOCS
This karate temple sure keeps us busy! Goddamn!
Damn, I love keeping ambulance drivers busy!
I haven't seen the inside of an ambulance in a LONG time!!!
What the FUCK?
I'd like to show you the inside of an ambulance!
Ha! I think I'll show the inside of an ambulance to YOU, instead!!!
So, what do you think of the inside of our ambulance?

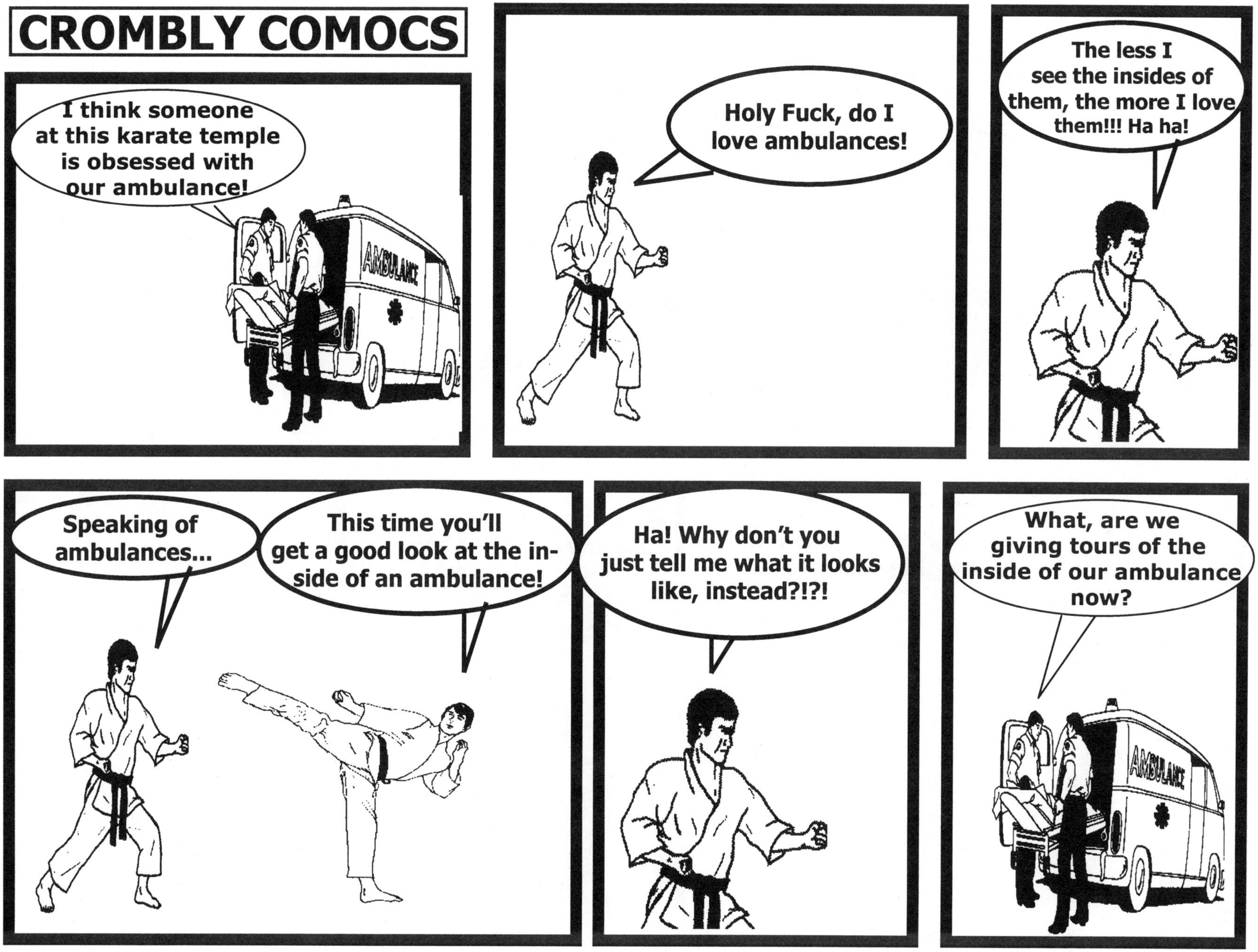
CROMBLY COMOCS
I think someone at this karate temple is obsessed with our ambulance!
Holy Fuck, do I love ambulances!
The less I see the insides of them, the more I love them!!! Ha ha!
Speaking of ambulances...
This time you'll get a good look at the in-side of an ambulance!
Ha! Why don't you just tell me what it looks like, instead?!?!
What, are we giving tours of the inside of our ambulance now?
AMBULANCE
AMBULANCE

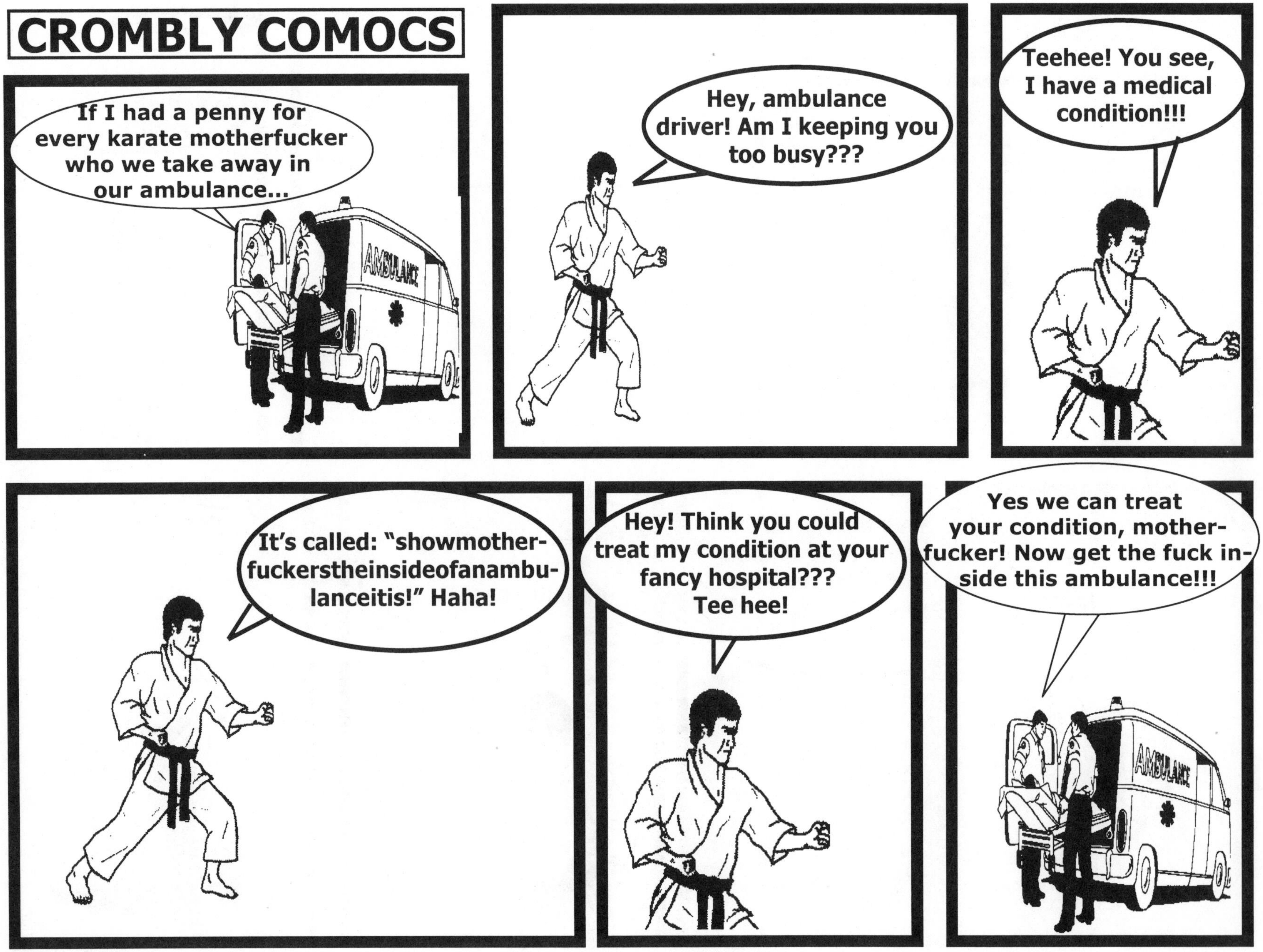
CROMBLY COMOCS
If I had a penny for every karate motherfucker who we take away in our ambulance...
AMBULANCE
Hey, ambulance driver! Am I keeping you too busy???
Teehee! You see, I have a medical condition!!!
It's called: "showmother-fuckerstheinsideofanambu-lanceitis!" Haha!
Hey! Think you could treat my condition at your fancy hospital??? Tee hee!
Yes we can treat your condition, mother-fucker! Now get the fuck in-side this ambulance!!!
AMBULANCE

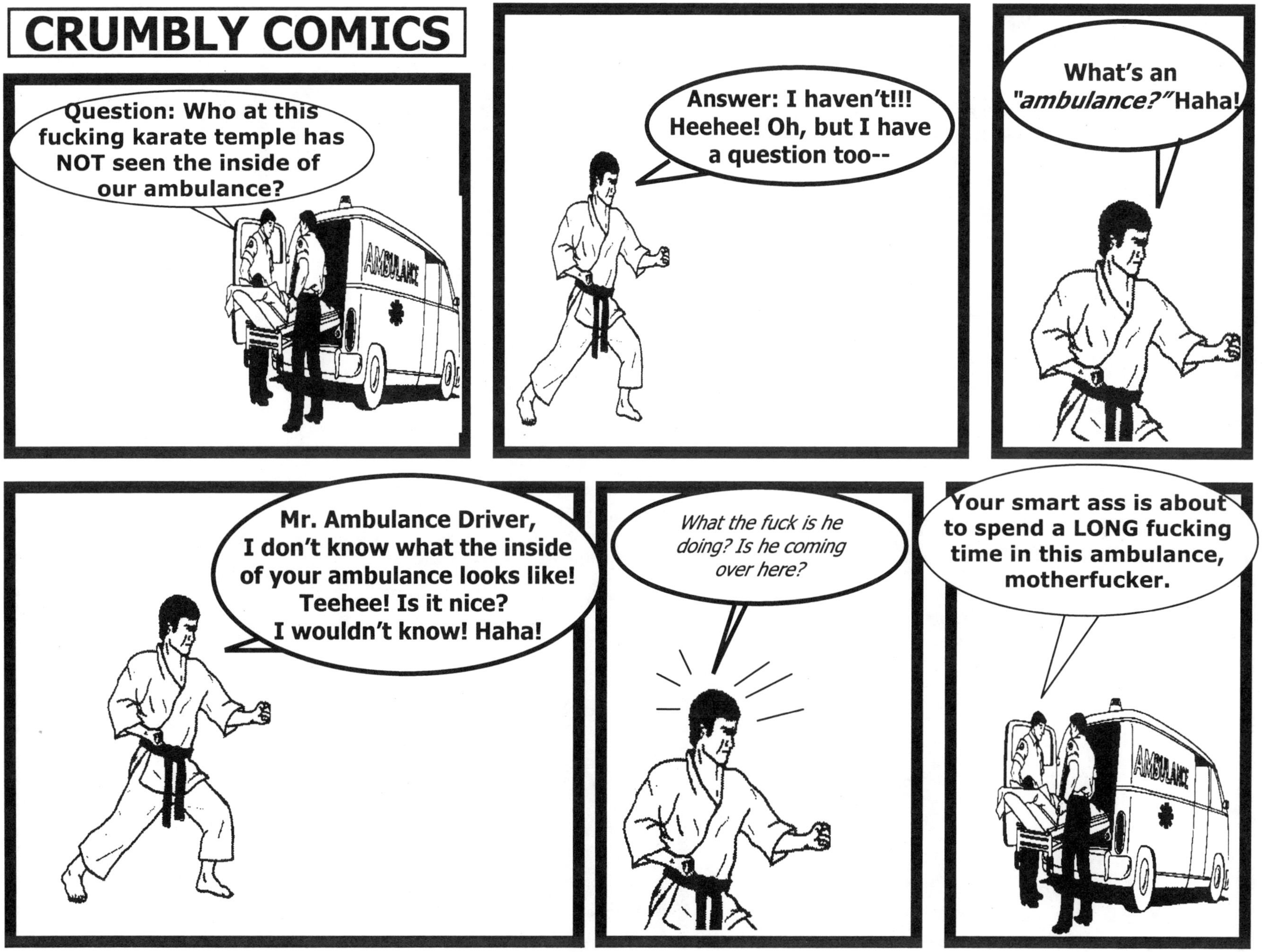
CRUMBLY COMICS
Question: Who at this fucking karate temple has NOT seen the inside of our ambulance?
Answer: I haven't!!! Heehee! Oh, but I have a question too--
What's an "ambulance?" Haha!
Mr. Ambulance Driver, I don't know what the inside of your ambulance looks like! Teehee! Is it nice? I wouldn't know! Haha!
What the fuck is he doing? Is he coming over here?
Your smart ass is about to spend a LONG fucking time in this ambulance, motherfucker.

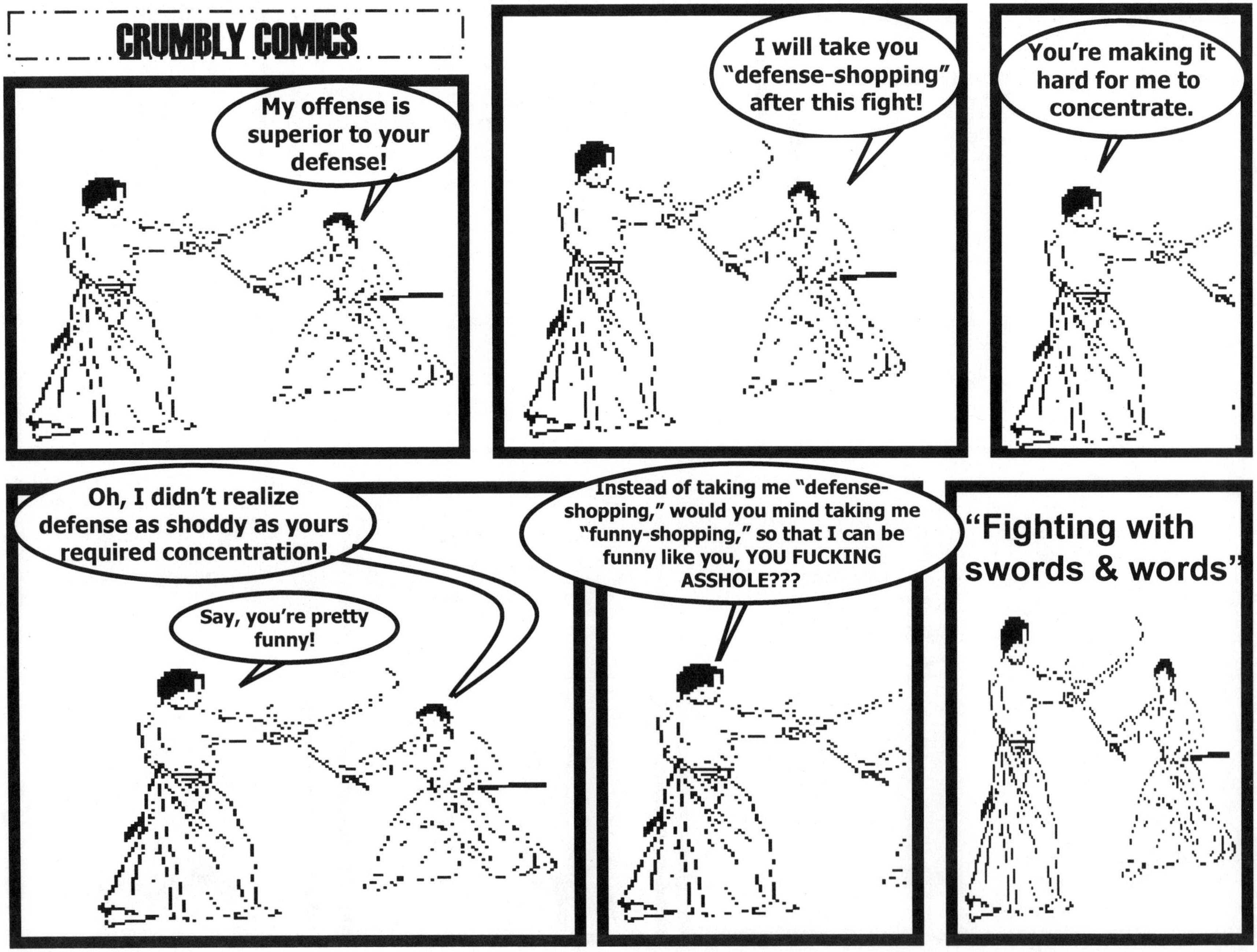
CRUMBLY COMICS
My offense is superior to your defense!
I will take you "defense-shopping" after this fight!
You're making it hard for me to concentrate.
Oh, I didn't realize defense as shoddy as yours required concentration!
Say, you're pretty funny!
Instead of taking me "defense-shopping," would you mind taking me "funny-shopping," so that I can be funny like you, YOU FUCKING ASSHOLE???
"Fighting with swords & words"

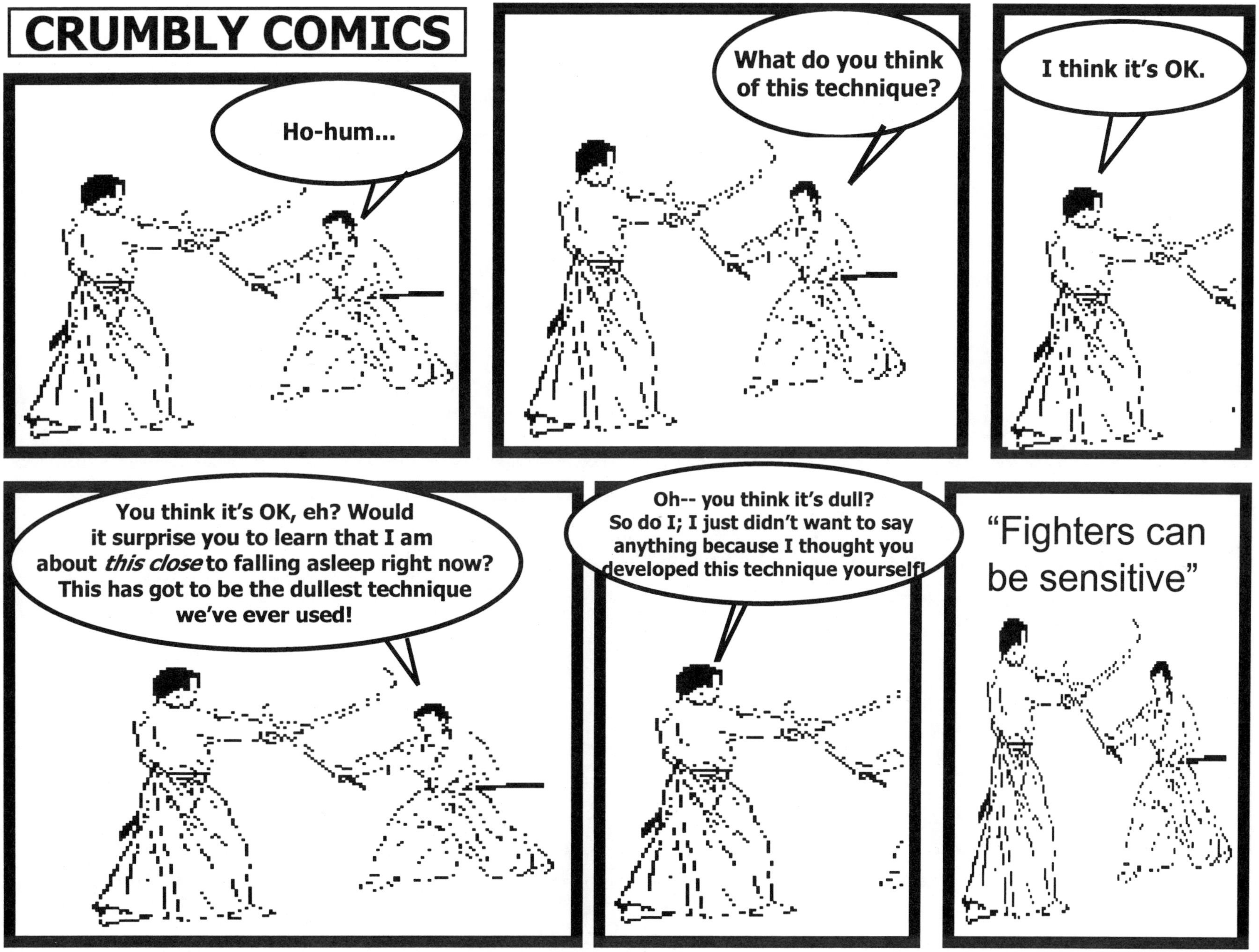
CRUMBLY COMICS
Ho-hum...
What do you think of this technique?
I think it's OK.
You think it's OK, eh? Would it surprise you to learn that I am about *this close* to falling asleep right now? This has got to be the dullest technique we've ever used!
Oh-- you think it's dull? So do I; I just didn't want to say anything because I thought you developed this technique yourself!
"Fighters can be sensitive"

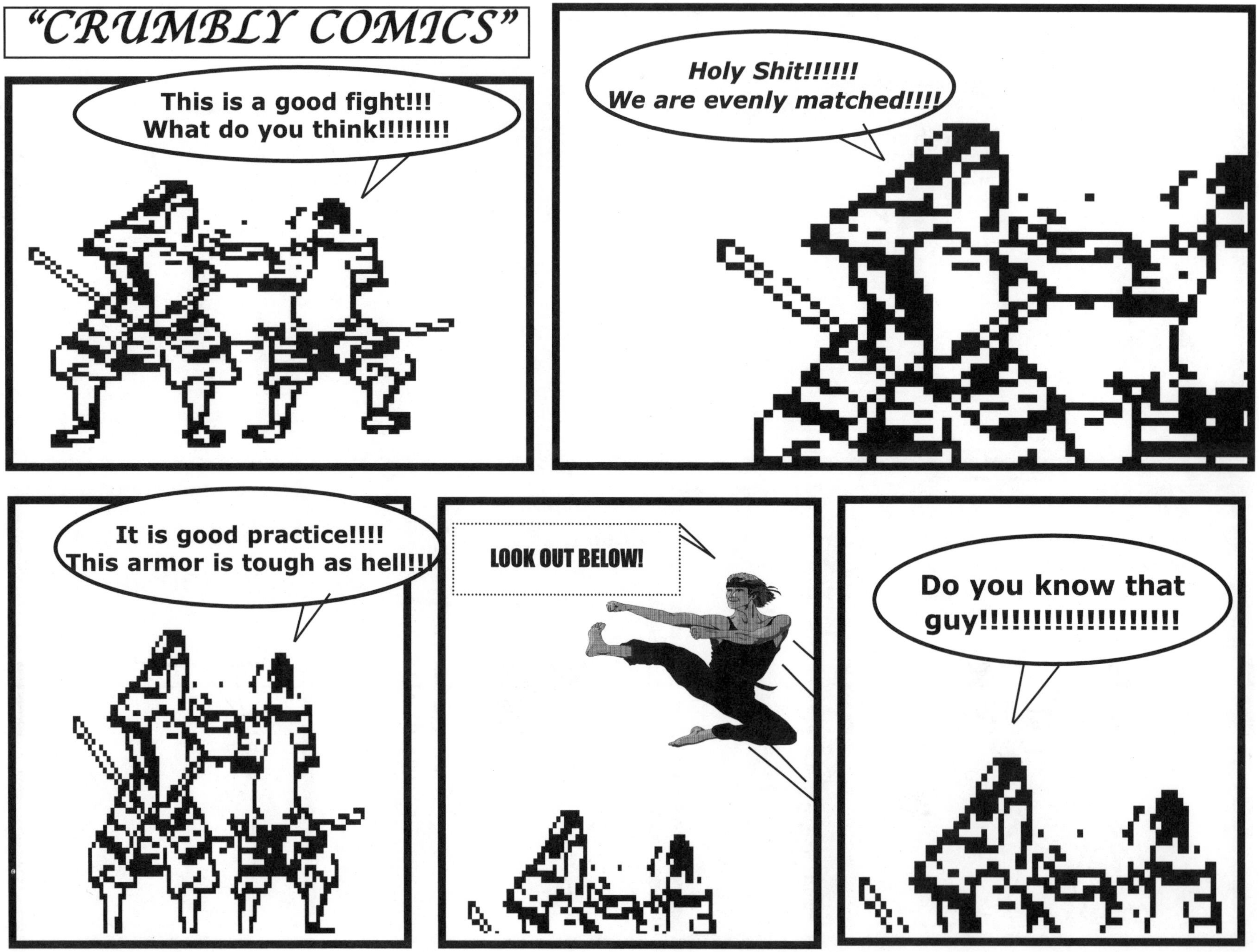
"CRUMBLY COMICS"
This is a good fight!!! What do you think!!!!!!!!
Holy Shit!!!!!! We are evenly matched!!!!
It is good practice!!!! This armor is tough as hell!!!
LOOK OUT BELOW!
Do you know that guy!!!!!!!!!!!!!!!!!!!

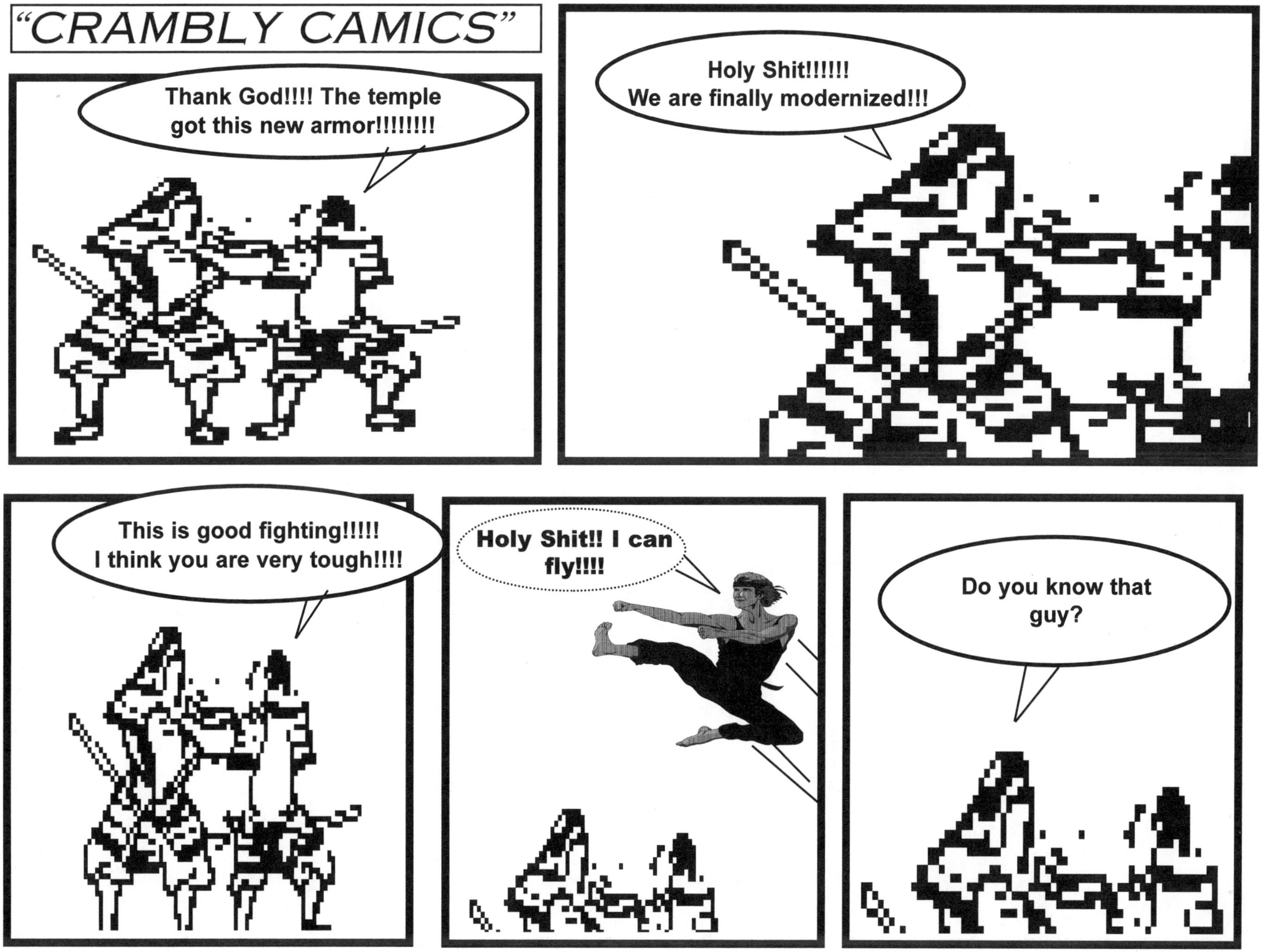
"CRAMBLY CAMICS"
Thank God!!!! The temple got this new armor!!!!!!!!
Holy Shit!!!!!!
We are finally modernized!!!
This is good fighting!!!!!
I think you are very tough!!!!
Holy Shit!! I can fly!!!!
Do you know that guy?

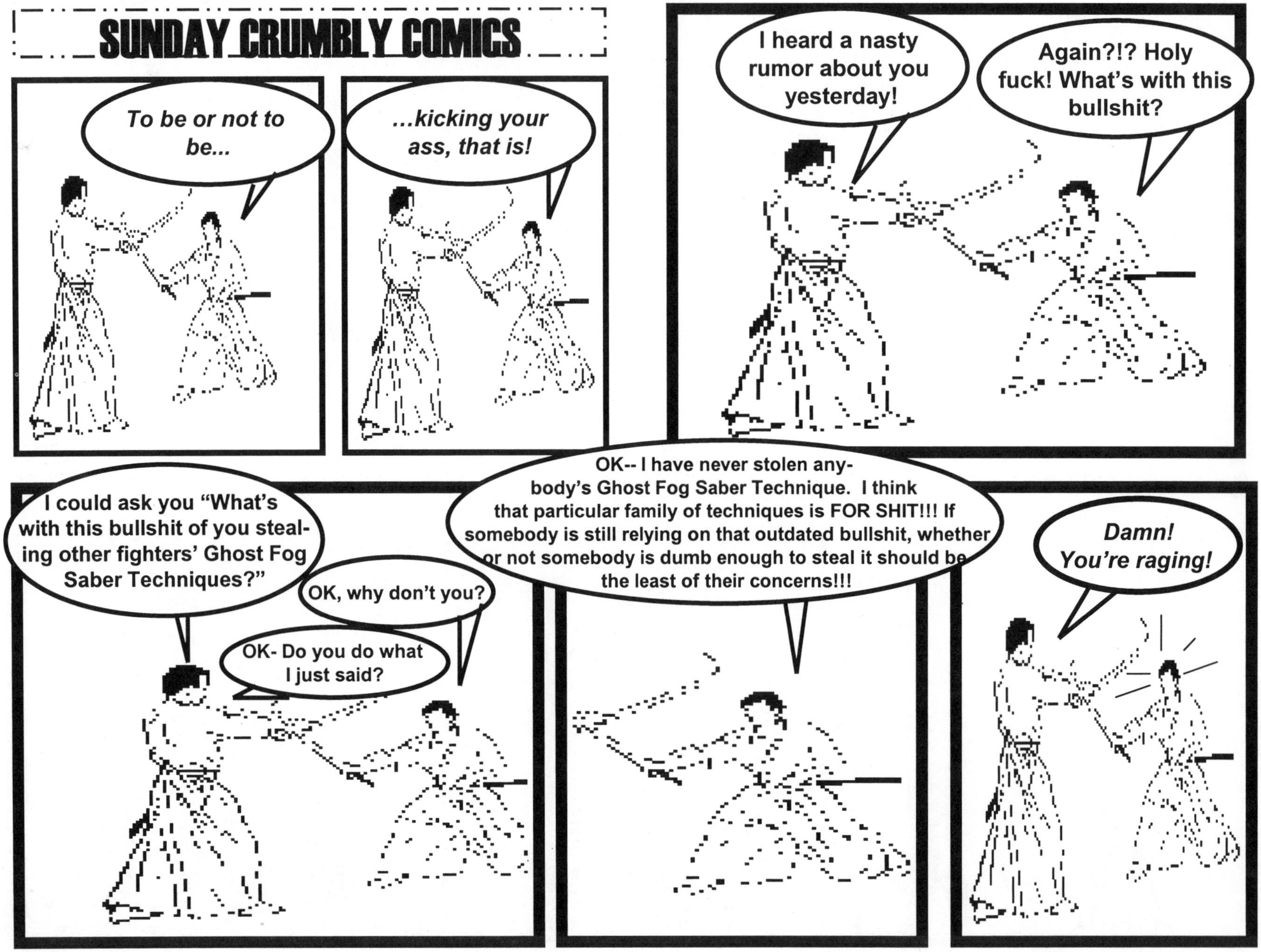
SUNDAY CRUMBLY COMICS
To be or not to be...
...kicking your ass, that is!
I heard a nasty rumor about you yesterday!
Again?!? Holy fuck! What's with this bullshit?
I could ask you "What's with this bullshit of you stealing other fighters' Ghost Fog Saber Techniques?"
OK, why don't you?
OK- Do you do what I just said?
OK-- I have never stolen anybody's Ghost Fog Saber Technique. I think that particular family of techniques is FOR SHIT!!! If somebody is still relying on that outdated bullshit, whether or not somebody is dumb enough to steal it should be the least of their concerns!!!
Damn! You're raging!

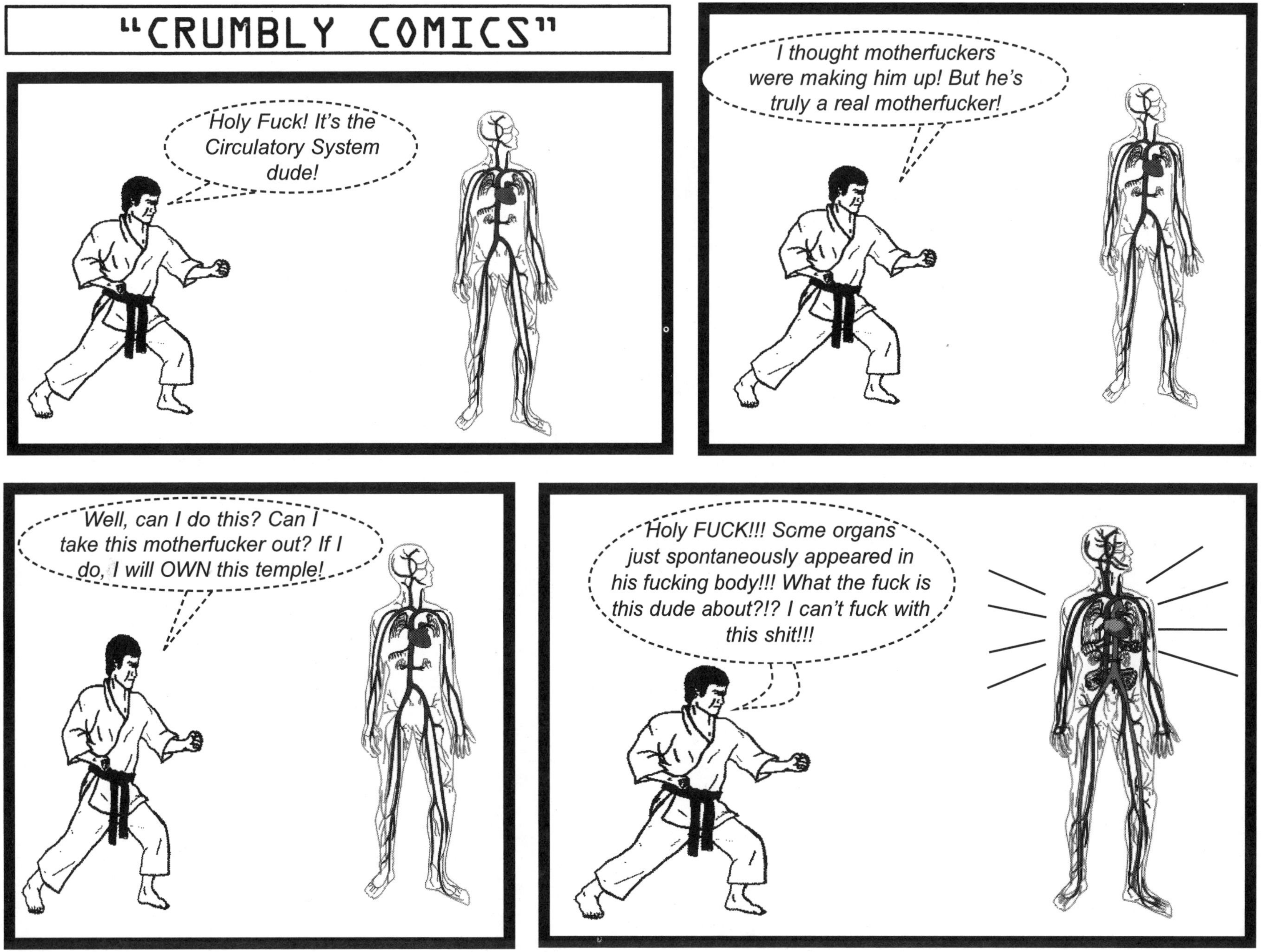
"CRUMBLY COMICS"
Holy Fuck! It's the Circulatory System dude!
I thought motherfuckers were making him up! But he's truly a real motherfucker!
Well, can I do this? Can I take this motherfucker out? If I do, I will OWN this temple!
Holy FUCK!!! Some organs just spontaneously appeared in his fucking body!!! What the fuck is this dude about?!? I can't fuck with this shit!!!

"CRUMBLY COMICS"
Holy Fuck! This motherfucker's back at the temple???
Can you believe this motherfucker?
Take a good look, dude. Because you will NEVER, NEVER be able to defeat this cat.
I can't believe it--- I can fucking see his goddamn internal organs. It's totally beyond reality!!!
Just take a good long look at the toughest motherfucker on the planet-- because you're not SHIT compared to this dude!
Holy-Living-Fuck!

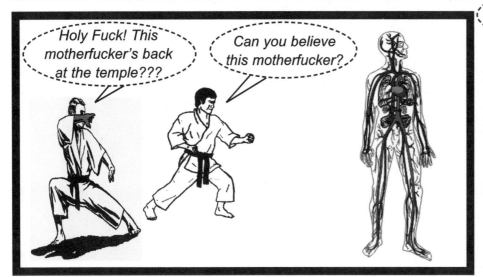

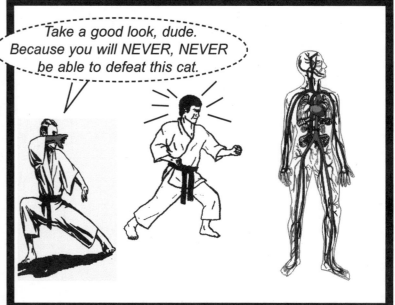

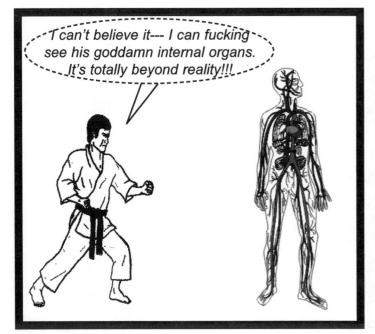

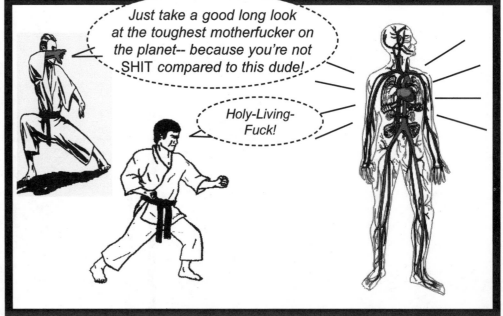

"CRUMBLY FUCKICS"
This shit is disturbing to me. The dude is just too much of a bad-ass.
Fuck it-- I'll take him out!!!
You have a fucking reality disorder. That's all I can say.
Why should I be intimidated by this motherfucker? For all I know he's not even physically solid!
Dude, you need to just go home and take a nap. Because you don't even register on this motherfucker's radar screen. *YOU CAN SEE HIS GODDAMN LIVER!!!*
HOLY SHIT!!! FUCK!!!!

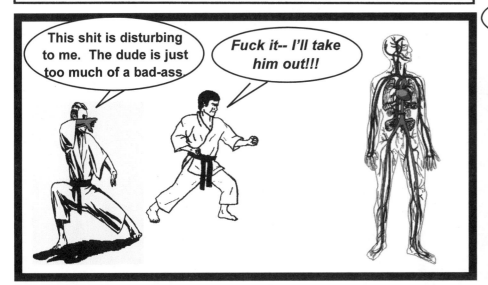

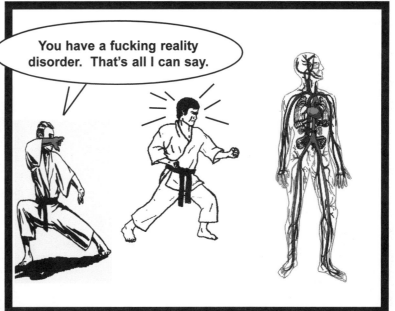

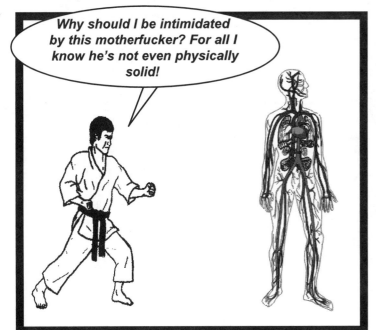

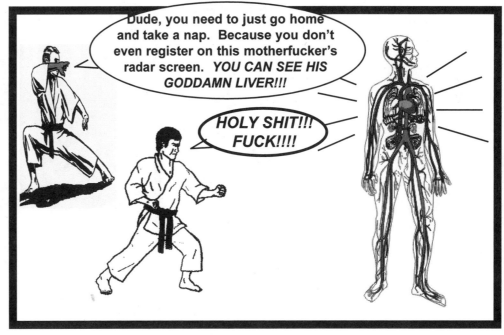

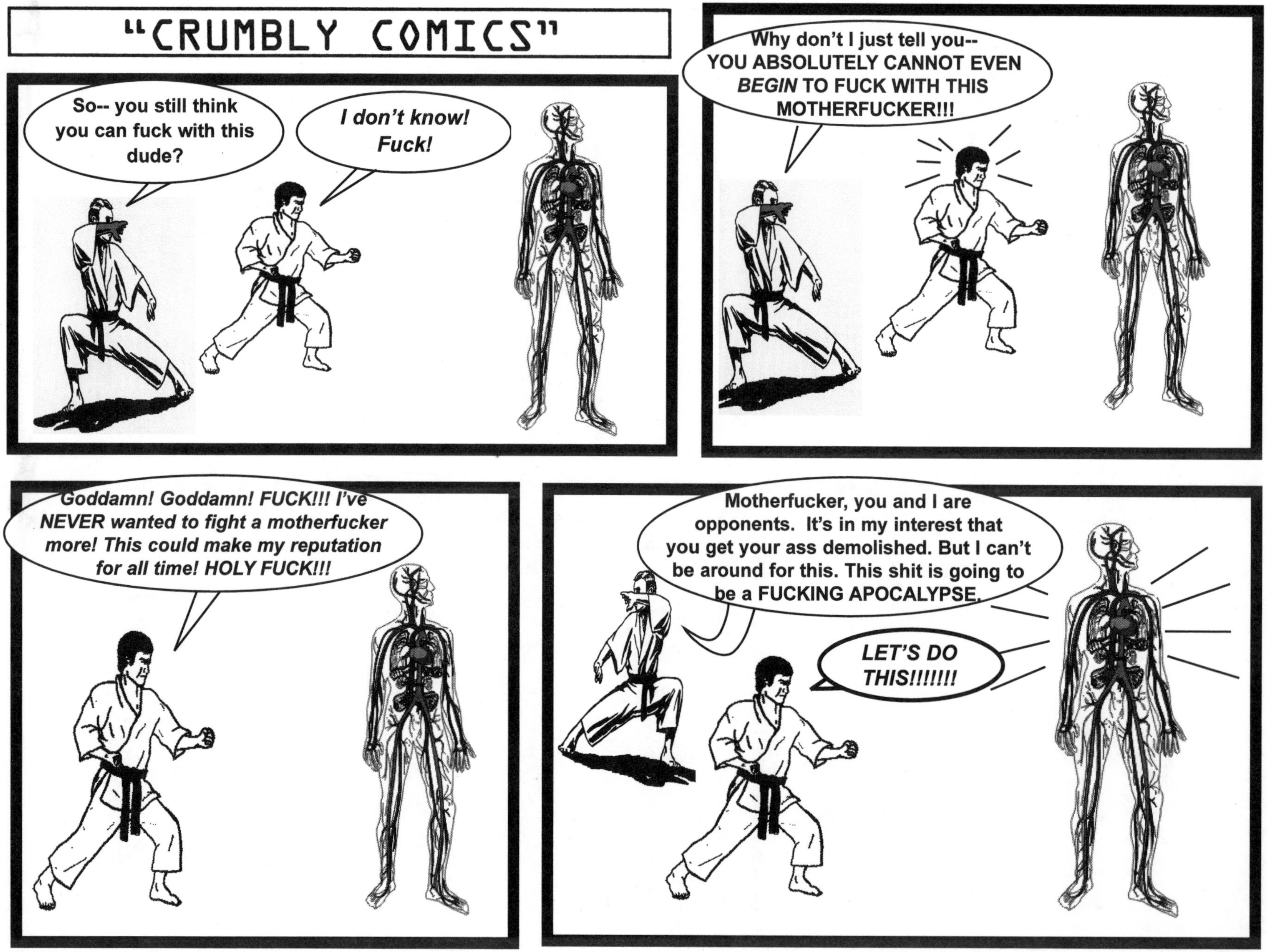
"CRUMBLY COMICS"
So-- you still think you can fuck with this dude?
I don't know! Fuck!
Why don't I just tell you-- YOU ABSOLUTELY CANNOT EVEN BEGIN TO FUCK WITH THIS MOTHERFUCKER!!!
Goddamn! Goddamn! FUCK!!! I've NEVER wanted to fight a motherfucker more! This could make my reputation for all time! HOLY FUCK!!!
Motherfucker, you and I are opponents. It's in my interest that you get your ass demolished. But I can't be around for this. This shit is going to be a FUCKING APOCALYPSE.
LET'S DO THIS!!!!!!!

"CRUMBLY COMICS"

AMBULANCE
AMBULANCE
AMBULANCE
Holy Fuck.
AMBULANCE

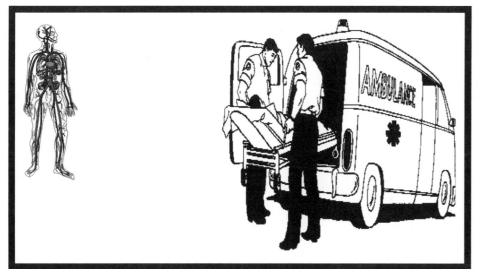

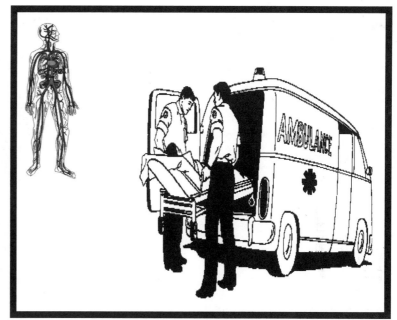

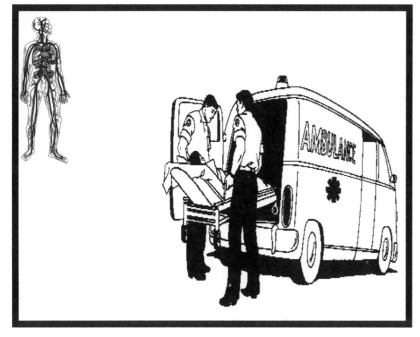

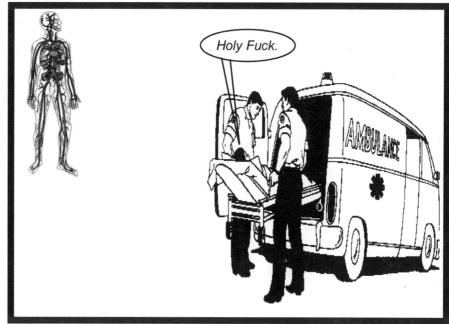

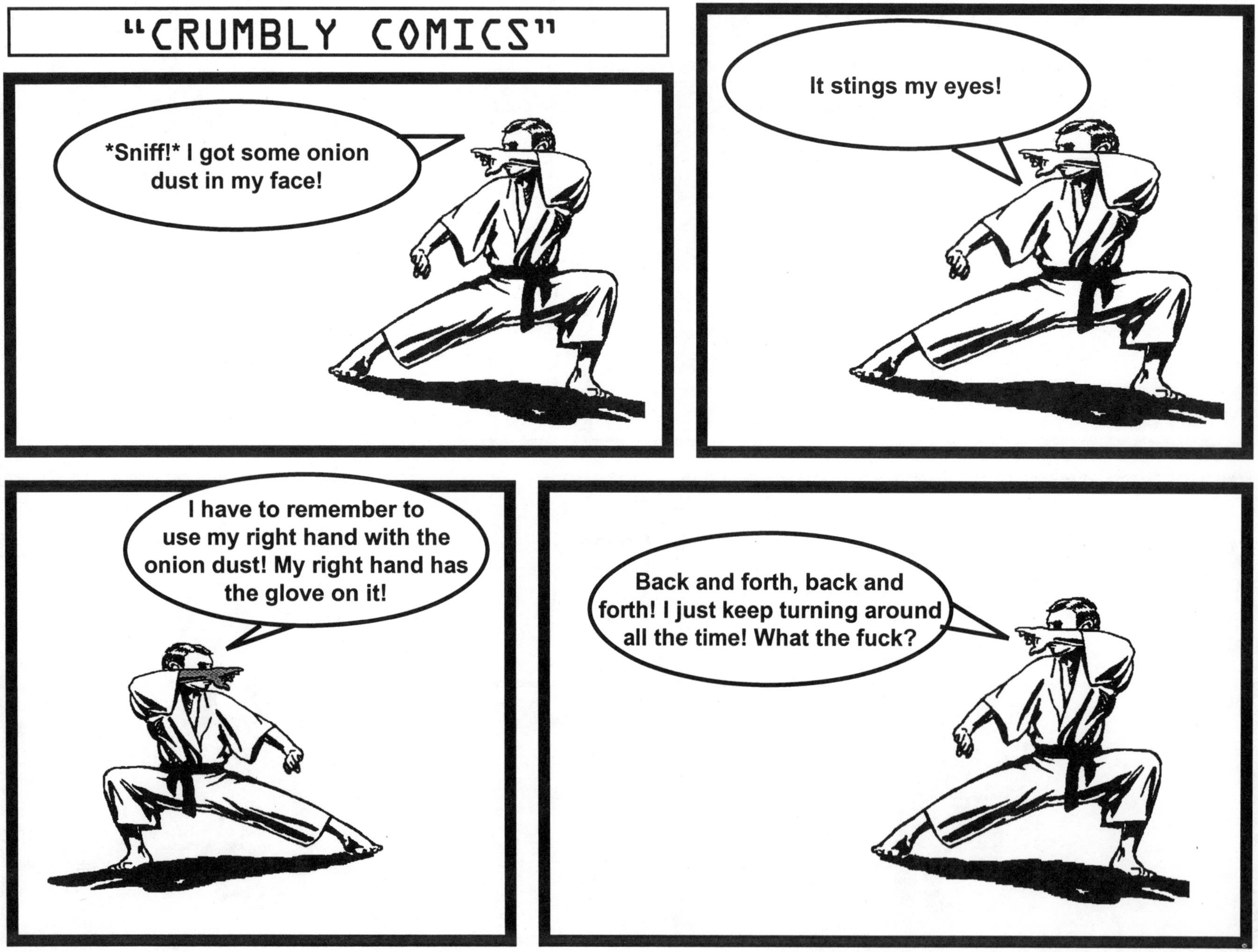
"CRUMBLY COMICS"
Sniff! I got some onion dust in my face!
It stings my eyes!
I have to remember to use my right hand with the onion dust! My right hand has the glove on it!
Back and forth, back and forth! I just keep turning around all the time! What the fuck?

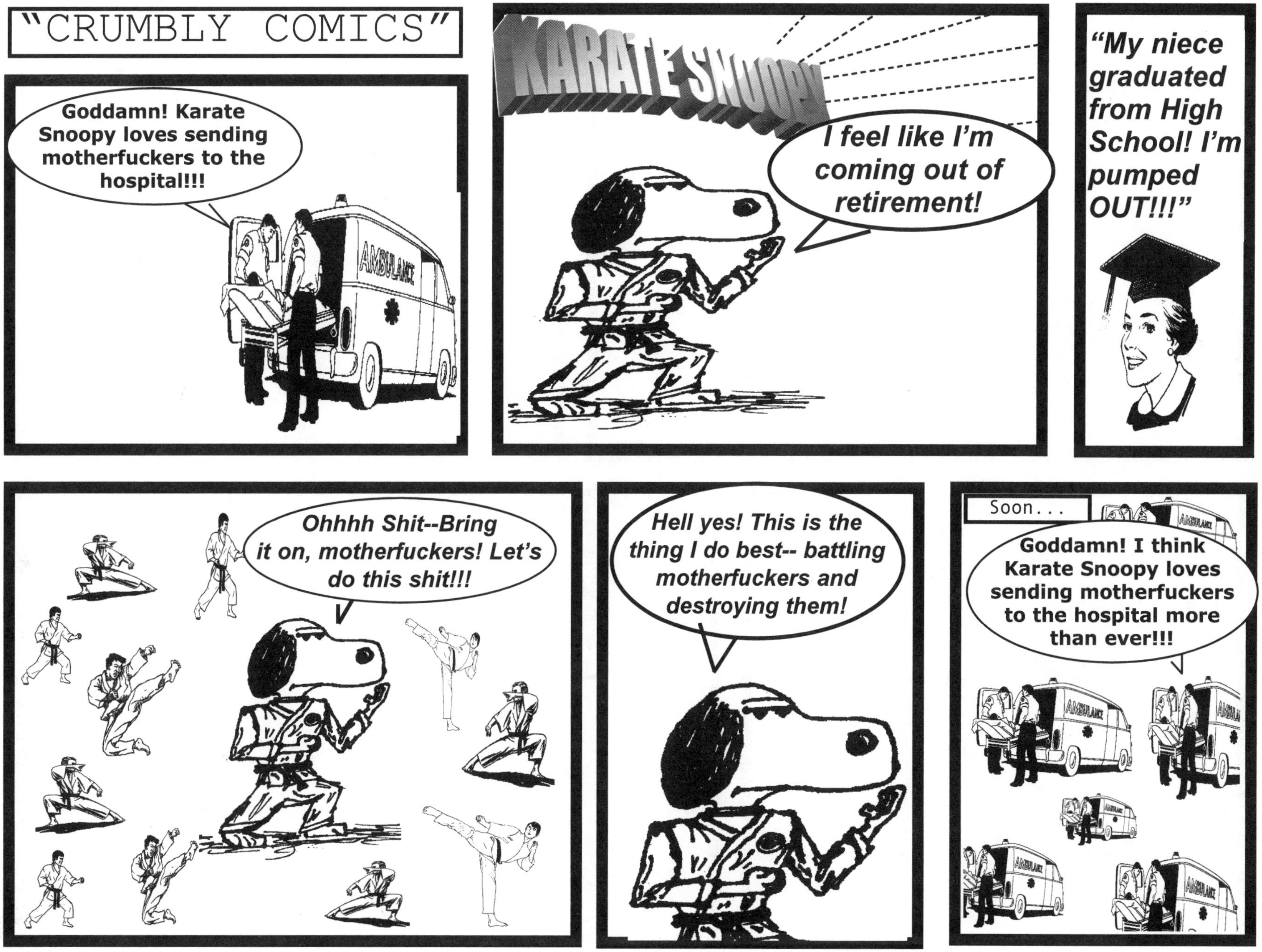
"CRUMBLY COMICS"
Goddamn! Karate Snoopy loves sending motherfuckers to the hospital!!!
AMBULANCE
KARATE SNOOPY
I feel like I'm coming out of retirement!
"My niece graduated from High School! I'm pumped OUT!!!"
Ohhhh Shit--Bring it on, motherfuckers! Let's do this shit!!!
Hell yes! This is the thing I do best-- battling motherfuckers and destroying them!
Soon...
Goddamn! I think Karate Snoopy loves sending motherfuckers to the hospital more than ever!!!

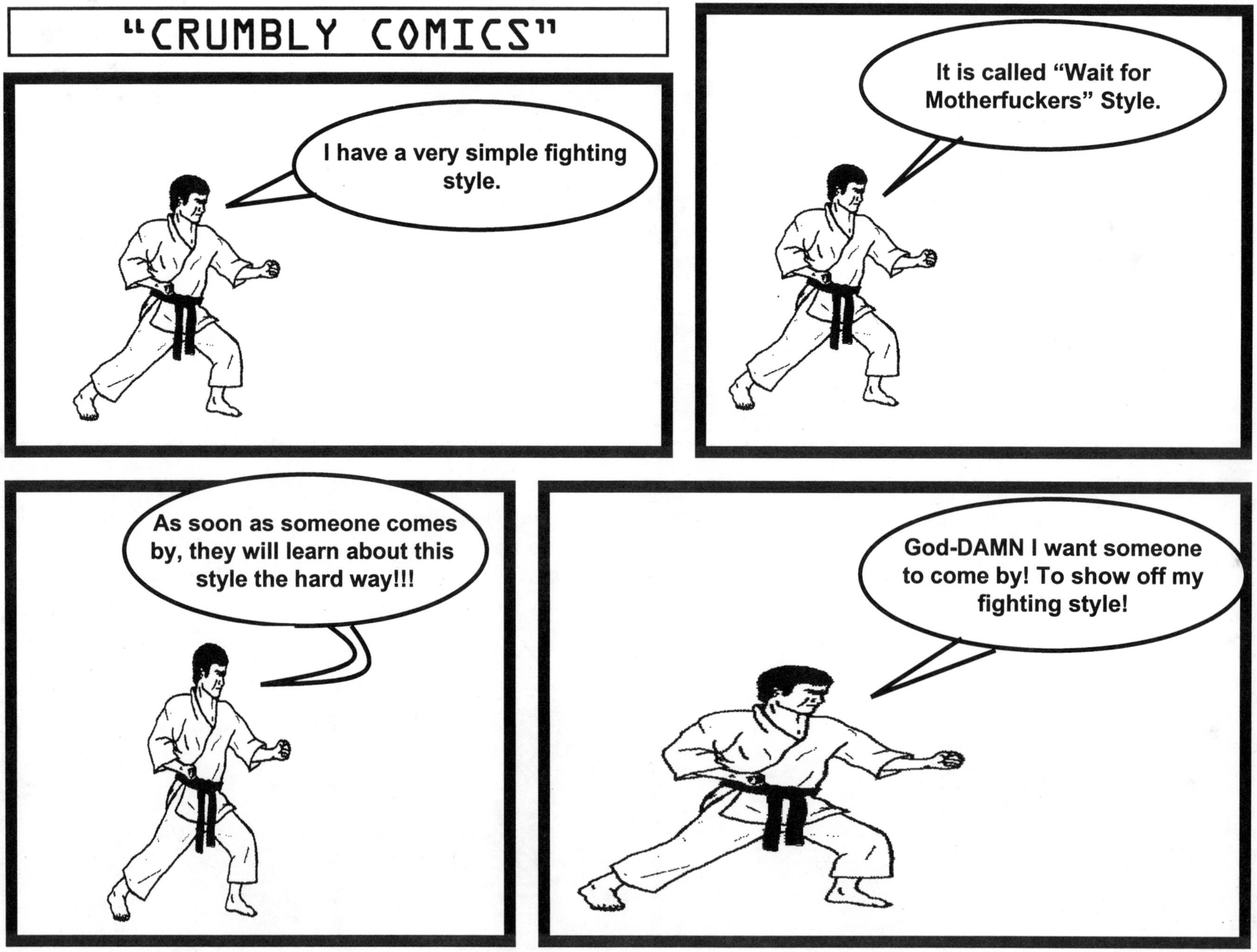
"CRUMBLY COMICS"
I have a very simple fighting style.
It is called "Wait for Motherfuckers" Style.
As soon as someone comes by, they will learn about this style the hard way!!!
God-DAMN I want someone to come by! To show off my fighting style!